"I have recently rediscovered a hymn that is quickly becoming my new favorite. The chorus is a repetitive 'O Christ, surround me. O Christ, surround me.' As I read Rev. McKibben Dana's book on hope, I found that refrain echoing in my spirit. Her words about hope surrounded me with a renewed sense of the presence of the Holy. She reminded me of the courage that has sat dormant in my spirit over these last couple of years. I will move forward with a deeper appreciation of how hope is an action and not just a feeling. (And goodness knows I love a good, subversive action!) By doing so, I anticipate being even more deeply immersed in the presence of God who always surrounds me. I am thankful for her persistent, consistent, wonderfully disruptive reclaiming of hope."

— SHANNON JOHNSON KERSHNER
pastor of Fourth Presbyterian Church, Chicago

"In an era when fear seems to have gained the upper hand, MaryAnn McKibben Dana has produced a much-needed 'user's manual' on hope. Drawing on her own rootedness in faith as well as personal experiences and keen insights on the human condition, MaryAnn's book lives up to its name. Anyone who needs motivation in these challenging and often discouraging times will find this volume, which includes reflective questions and suggestions for action at the end of each chapter, a helpful tool. MaryAnn openly shares her own struggles in a disarming way, and provides strategies for faithful, hope-filled living in a style remarkably free of 'churchy' or theological language. I highly recommend this book to those who need encouragement to 'keep on keeping on.' Perhaps that includes all of us!"

— CHARLES YOOST
senior director of religious life and pastoral care at
Lakeside Chautauqua, Ohio

Hope

- A User's Manual -

MaryAnn McKibben Dana

William B. Eerdmans Publishing Company
Grand Rapids, Michigan

Wm. B. Eerdmans Publishing Co.
4035 Park East Court SE, Grand Rapids, Michigan 49546
www.eerdmans.com

28 27 26 25 24 23   4 5 6 7 8

ISBN 978-0-8028-8231-8

Library of Congress Cataloging-in-Publication Data

A catalog record for this book is available from the Library of Congress.

Contents

~-~

Acknowledgments

THIS BOOK WAS WRITTEN while living through a pandemic.

As such, I'm grateful to everyone who supported MaryAnn the Human, not just MaryAnn the Author, during this time. Thanks to you, I didn't just *get* through it, I *moved* through it (see p. 156), which gave this book the space and grace to happen. Special thanks to my extended family—mother, siblings, aunts, uncles, cousins, nieblings—and all of our Zooms, movie discussions, and holiday music drafts. Thank you to The Well, especially Thirsty Thursdays; the CGs, who always had the right meme at the right time; Trinity Presbyterian Church in Herndon, VA, for your unglamorous yet joyful work in service to the way of Jesus; LeAnn Hodges, for weekly accountability; and Marilyn Williams, for a veritable blitzkrieg of truth bombs over the years.

A lot of this book grew out of blog posts, newsletter articles, conversations, and monthly Hope Notes gatherings. If you partook of any of these, and especially if you replied, commented, questioned, or said "same here," you are a part of this book.

My coaching clients teach me so much. Thanks for giving me a front-row seat for your brilliant wrestling. Your wisdom is all over these pages as well.

Peruse this book's quotes and footnotes, and you'll find an extensive array of folks who deserve my gratitude as well, but I especially want to shout out Cathy Bonczek, Derrick Weston, Becca Messman, and Chris

Tuttle. Matthew McKibben, your nerdery was invaluable, especially for the story section. Thanks for helping me light the beacons.

Many thanks to the Louisville Institute for the gift of a Pastoral Study Project grant; to the Porches Writing Retreat in Norwood, VA, for the hospitality when things were coming down to the wire; and to the folks at Eerdmans, especially David Bratt, Andrew Knapp, and Laurel Draper, for helping guide this book into its final form.

Robert Dana, you're such a good human. Caroline Dana, you survived hell, and a beautiful life is yours to embrace. Mel Dana, I'm so grateful for your creativity, your strength, and your heart. James Dana, buddy, thank you for the walks and the laughs. I love you all. I love you each.

Introduction

I REMEMBER EXACTLY when this book began to take shape in my mind and heart.

A few years ago, I was coaching a pastor who served a small congregation. Aaron (not his real name) had labored long and well to lead this tiny band of scrappy, social-justice-oriented folks in a medium-sized town in the Bible Belt. When he began his time there, he felt energized and full of can-do hopefulness that the church would thrive under his leadership. Over the subsequent years he saw evangelical churches flourish all around him, while his small flock continued to do its thing—faithfully, but without much glitz or fanfare, and without much growth either. In fact, like many aging congregations, their numbers declined year by year, the financial coffers were depleted, and Aaron grew increasingly exhausted. Over time, his sense of hope eroded, and he felt stuck.

The conversation turned to that quote from Mother Teresa, popular in ministry circles, that we're called not necessarily to be successful, but to be faithful. Aaron said something like, "I remember learning that in seminary, and have seen it referenced many times since. But there's an unspoken part of it, which is that if you're faithful, you'll be successful. You can't be 'in it' for the success, however you define it. But it will come if you do it right. It's like we're all captive to this unspoken equation: so long as you have enough hope and do your best, things will work out. And it's a lie. It's just a lie."

Yes, it is.

It's a lie that's rampant in American Christianity—indeed, in American culture:

We can do anything if we put our minds to it.
If you believe hard enough, things will work out just as you hope.
Input ABC, output XYZ.

Reality is much more complicated. We can do everything "right" and things still may not turn out as we'd like. Aaron named a harsh truth: many of us grind it out, clinging to the myth of inexorable progress and calling that "hope," but it's anything but.

That kind of hope falls short when things are bleak—which is when we need hope the most.

How do we cultivate hope to face each day, even when our efforts don't bear fruit? How do people like Aaron and the community he serves find the energy to persevere, knowing that their efforts may not end in triumph but in a slow decline into an eventual closure? For that matter, how do we pursue the work of justice, knowing that the task is too big for any of us?

This book is an attempt to address these questions and to write myself back into a sense of hope.

It's been a tumultuous few years for myself, my family, and the world. Though this is not a pandemic book, you will see COVID-19's hulking presence from time to time, as well as the looming specter of climate change, and the urgent work of confronting racial and economic injustice.

Also braided throughout these pages is our family's experience walking with our daughter through a debilitating depression that extended over a couple of years of high school. Where possible, I try to keep the focus on my experience; my daughter's story is not mine to tell. Even when I may overshoot that boundary, be assured that Caroline has read every word and given approval to the words that appear here.

In writing this book, I found hope hiding in the nooks and crannies of my kid's depression journey. But as you'll discover, it's also lurking in tattooed wisdom from a beloved children's book and in Marvel movies; on the running trail and in a sweater full of holes. Notably, hope is present in the experience of marginalized communities and among people of color, who've found their way into a hope that's quite different from the one I've coasted on for most of my life as a White woman of relative privilege.

And hope is present for me in the faith I claim as a pastor in the Christian tradition, a tradition I cannot quit but with which I have a perpetual lovers' quarrel. This book is for religious folk who, like me, are weary of pat answers and scripty-font platitudes about hope. It's for seekers who've left the church, and for those who've never entered but are curious and open to constructing a spiritual life that matters. It's for anyone who's ready for a hope that's scrappy and durable, and who *may* find inspiration in sacred texts but also find it readily in pop culture, literature, and art. It's for people who are dizzy from the apostle Paul's rigid merry-go-round of suffering producing endurance producing character producing hope (Romans 5) and for those who'd never ever buy a ticket for that ride.

Too often, hope is the stuff of Instagram memes, pithy enough to fit in a perfect square, rendered in elegant, sans serif type. But true hope resists such reductions. This is a user's manual in the sense that you're meant to *do* something with what you read, but you will find no step-by-step instructions here.

I've organized the book into six sections. Section 1, "What Hope Is Not," will knock down some of the most common misconceptions about hope. Section 2, "What Hope Is," offers a few ways of thinking about hope to replace what we've dismantled. Section 3, "Hope Lives in the Body," explores the messiness of our imperfect, flawed, beautiful human bodies and argues that when we care for ourselves, we allow hope to thrive. Section 4, "Hope Travels in Story," delves into the idea that hope is not a process or a set of goals but a narrative in which we live and move.

Section 5, "The Practice of Hope," offers some tangible ways to cultivate hope even in hopeless times. It's the most tactical part of the book, though even there you won't find procedures and checklists so much as experiments. And section 6, "Hope Beyond Hope," offers thoughts about how we persevere, both when we're feeling hopeful and when we're not.

Within each section are short reflections that relate to the section's theme but that also stand alone. You could easily skip around the book, just like you would with any user's manual or reference guide. The reflections are brief enough for you to gobble them up, binge-reading style, but I hope you won't. As you read each one, I encourage you to pause and consider questions such as:

- What is resonating with you?
- Where are you experiencing resistance?
- What are you feeling invited to do, think, or feel?

You've probably seen the line emblazoned on posters and paperweights: What would you do if you knew you could not fail?

When the world's on fire, a better question may be: What is worth doing even if you think you will fail?

Once we can answer that question, we'll be in touch with a hope that cannot fail us.

Let us begin.

1

What Hope Is Not

When it comes to hope, our culture peddles a lot of cheap knockoffs.

This section of our user's manual invites us to clean out the toolbox, removing all those dull and rusty tools that don't work for us anymore.

As you read these reflections, take time to rummage through your own life. Are any of these ideas present? How do they help you access hope? How do they get in the way of hope?

⌒

BEFORE THERE WAS YouTube, Instagram, or TikTok, there was public access television.

When I was a high schooler, I participated in a Great Books discussion with a group of classmates as part of an afternoon enrichment program. We met regularly to read short passages from works of literature and analyze them. For reasons lost to time, and to my great bafflement both then and now, one of these discussions was recorded for a local-access channel. We reported to an actual studio and attempted to do there what we normally did in a classroom after school. We sat at long, heavy, conference style tables. Lights glared in our faces, rendering the rest of the room pitch dark. I wore a nice dress—solid colored, no print, as I'd been instructed by the producer via our faculty sponsor.

For the discussion, we were given a short portion of *Robinson Crusoe*, Daniel Defoe's novel about a man who's shipwrecked and alone (he presumes) on an island. The excerpt included a diary entry in which Crusoe detailed some problems he'd solved that allowed him to survive more easily. He salvaged supplies from the ship; he made candles. The question for discussion was, "Does Crusoe feel hopeful or hopeless about his situation of being shipwrecked?"

One by one, my fellow students argued one side or the other, citing various bits in the passage to support their assertions. I listened with a mounting sense of alarm. For one thing, there was a huge camera with a blinking light right in front of me, examining me as if with a huge judgmental eye. (Perhaps I overestimated the number of people who would watch a bunch of fourteen-year-olds on public access.) But also, I couldn't decide which way I wanted to argue, and a big part of me didn't want to take a side. But everyone else did.

Finally it was my turn. I said something like this: *It depends. It depends on what we think the "situation" is. Is it rescue, or is it survival? Does he have hope for ever being rescued? No, it doesn't seem like it. But it seems like he's hopeful that he can live well and in good health for quite some time. So . . . it depends.*

I felt dumb for not being able to take a firm position like everyone else. But as I would learn years later in college, the answer to the question depends on how we frame it. Mostly, though, middle-aged me wants to put a sisterly arm around that awkward teen in the solid-not-print dress because she stumbled on something important, maybe even a core belief: that hope is often more general than specific, more internally oriented than outwardly predictive. Crusoe doesn't know whether he will be found; how can he know? What he does know is, he's built a shelter for himself and a cellar for food. He's found goats he can butcher for meat. He's resilient, to use a word much more common in the twenty-first century than the eighteenth when the novel was written. He's relatively comfortable and he's alive.

When we say we're hopeful, we often follow it with a "that."

I'm hopeful that the chemo will work.

I'm hopeful that I'll find a job soon.

I'm hopeful that the new meds will help curb the depression.

There's nothing wrong with hope that points in a particular direction. But when the world is falling apart, it can be hard to find a suitable "that" to complete the sentence. I have a friend who's worked on climate change on the local level for many years. Her organization has made clear but modest progress on a number of small initiatives. But she doesn't feel any hope that humans will act quickly and broadly enough to stem the tide of the catastrophe that's coming.

What then? Can we still have hope if the facts argue against it? How? Is hope possible even if we aren't attached to a particular outcome? The rest of this book will help us address this question, though maybe not answer it definitively.

But Cornel West says yes. The professor and activist borrows from the blues, a tradition that acknowledges the pain and glory of the present moment but doesn't revolve around a clear and chipper *that* in order to persevere. "A blues man is a prisoner of hope," he says. "Hope wrestles with despair. . . . It generates this energy to be courageous, to bear witness, to see what the end is going to be. No guarantee, unfinished, open-ended. I'm a prisoner of hope. I'm going to die full of hope."[1]

In almost forty years since that Great Books discussion, including four as an English major, I haven't read *Robinson Crusoe* beyond what appeared on that single photocopied sheet of paper. I don't know what becomes of the titular character. I doubt he's a blues man. But we can learn to be blues people. Our first step is to divorce "hope" from "that" . . . to embrace hope as mysterious and open ended and see where that takes us.

Reflect

Do you consider yourself a hopeful person? Why or why not, or in what circumstances?

Practice

Write a hope poem using all or some of these prompts:

Hope looks like . . .
Hope sounds like . . .
I hope that . . .
I hope despite . . .
Hope draws near when . . .
Hope feels far away when . . .

~~~~~~

I DECIDED TO DROP OFF a little something for a friend while driving through his town on a long road trip. His young son was in a health crisis and I wanted him to know I was thinking of him. I didn't call beforehand, unsure of my timing and not wanting to create an expectation that he work around my schedule. When I arrived, my friend's mother-in-law came to the door and accepted my small token. My inadequate token. She said, "They're actually at the doctor right now, confirming the diagnosis."

As I left, the memories came in a rush of the many people I've known who've experienced that Before-and-After moment. I've had a few of them myself, when things look bad, but you don't yet know how bad because it's still the Before. You cross your fingers, and maybe you pray. You do a little bargaining with the universe. You analyze the facts, scrutinizing the data from every angle, blurring your eyes if you have to, like with one of those hidden 3D pictures, to convince yourself that maybe it won't be as bad as you think. And then comes the After. And it is.

In talking to people about hope, I find one of the biggest sticking points is the distinction between hope and optimism. Many folks use the terms interchangeably. But there's a vital difference. Optimism does its best work in the Before—when the evidence points plausibly in a positive direction, when you can still anticipate the best possible outcome, when things could work out OK. But when the facts suggest otherwise, optimism isn't enough. This is when hope comes in, rolls up her sleeves and says, "Optimism, take a seat."

I've heard optimism described as a mathematical construct, an equation in which past experience + present striving = future greatness. Optimism relies on external circumstances lining up a certain way. Hope isn't mathematical; it's philosophical, physical, maybe even musical. True hope defies cause and effect and has impact regardless of outcome.

Having seen the facts and reports from every organization studying the climate, I have no optimism about avoiding the ravages of climate collapse. When the worst comes to pass, I don't know whether people will rise to the occasion or if there will be enough of us to blunt the full horrific impact. But I know that's the work I have to do: to embody that kind of hope. As Rabbi Jonathan Sacks says, "Optimism and hope are not the same. Optimism is the belief that the world is changing for the better; hope is the belief that, together, we can make the world better."[1]

It's understandable that hope and optimism would be so easily conflated, especially in the United States, which seems to lift up optimism as a civic virtue. That optimism has been a source of inspiration and innovation both here and abroad. But recent events are testing the tensile strength of optimism. The trajectory of unchecked, unfettered growth seems virtuous and unstoppable, until the ecosystem collapses and staggering inequality threatens our social fabric. American-style democracy seems inevitable because the Cold War ended and we won . . . until anti-democratic insurrectionists breach our own Capitol and we realize how fragile the whole enterprise truly is. Too often, optimism serves as a kind of autopilot at a time when we need to be scrupulously minding the controls.

At this point I need to pause and clarify the "we" who possess all this historical optimism. Thanks to conversations with Black friends and other people of color, I understand the extent to which optimism is a largely White or privileged phenomenon. It's easy to put your trust in things working out OK when they typically have. As Chris de la Cruz writes:

American optimism and positivity may have helped individuals cope with some of the stresses of our over-worked, capitalistic system. But did these mechanisms just help us soothe ourselves enough so that people don't adequately process how inhuman and unjust the modern systems are, and therefore not stir the drive and desire to change the system itself? Rich people are optimistic that "things will work out" because they in fact always do – because they have rigged the system to make it so.[2]

To be clear, many members of marginalized communities and people of color feel hopeful, but if they do, it's often in spite of the facts on the ground, and unbuoyed by optimism.

The good news is, no matter who we are, hope is a muscle that can be exercised. Research shows that hopeful people have access to two kinds of thinking that merely optimistic ones don't. The first is called "pathway thinking," which allows people to imagine many possible approaches to a situation in pursuit of a goal or outcome. The second, "agency thinking," is a sense of personal empowerment and motivation to work to pursue those goals or outcomes. Pathway thinking dreams of many potential futures; agency thinking tries to bring them about.[3]

My therapist has a personal mantra she's been kind enough to let me borrow: *I know there's another way to look at this.* That's hopeful, pathway thinking at work.

"Another way to look at this" doesn't give us license to gaslight ourselves when bad things happen. Sometimes things just suck. But a hopeful orientation ruminates, turning the situation over and over, refusing to give up on possibility. Meanwhile the poor optimist, bound by circumstance, has nowhere to go.

Reflect

How do you understand the difference between hope and optimism? Do you consider yourself a hopeful person? An optimistic person? Is one a requirement for the other?

Practice

Think about a situation in your life that requires hope. Practice pathway thinking: imagine as many possible outcomes or solutions as you can. Don't worry about how realistic they are—go for quantity over quality. Then practice agency thinking: develop a phrase or mantra to help remember that even when we get overwhelmed, there is always something we can control, however small it might seem.

OF THE SEVEN THOUSAND LANGUAGES currently spoken around the world, a shocking number are vulnerable to extinction, with one language dying every two weeks.[1] Thankfully there's a desperate and beautiful movement afoot to learn and document as many of them as possible. One of these documentary efforts has occurred among the Aymara people in Bolivia, Peru, and northern Chile. Anthropologists have long sought to learn the people's idioms, and in their study, they discovered a peculiar feature. Specifically, the Aymara speak of past and future in very different ways than the researchers' home customs. The Aymara word for past is *nayra*, which literally means "eye," "sight," or "front." The word for future is *q'ipa*, which translates as "behind" or "the back."[2]

Language is more than words; it is also gestures, and when describing events that take place in the past, the Aymara reinforce the word by gesturing in front of their body. In fact, the further in the past they're describing, the more they extend their arm in front of them, as if drawing out an imaginary timeline. Future events, by contrast, prompt a gesture over the person's shoulder, as if tossing an imaginary object behind them.

The reasoning goes like this: The past, as a completed set of events, is known. We can glimpse it. It's as clear as whatever's in front of our face. The future, by contrast, is unknown, and therefore hidden, like whatever lurks behind us that we can't see.

To put it mildly, we do things differently here in the United States and in many other Western countries. The past is *behind* us, discarded;

the future is *in front of us*, ours to claim. This mentality is so endemic to
our cultural psyche that it's hard to imagine such statements without
exclamation points.

Put your past behind you!
Charge into the future!

We see ourselves perpetually standing on the precipice of our potential, moving ever toward it. The past recedes behind our backs as we
hurtle forward.

American English is far from the only language that frames the past
as behind us and the future on the path ahead, ripe for the taking. But
perhaps we have perfected the concept. It's embedded in our own complicated history. We landed on a continent we saw as ours to claim. We
threw off the yoke of monarchical rule. We went west as our so-called
manifest destiny, subduing both the land and the people living on it.

The echoes of that ethos persist today. Immigrants to this country
are encouraged to learn English, to assimilate to "our" culture. Less than
40 percent of us live in the towns where we grew up, opting to seek our
fortunes and pursue our happiness in far-flung places. Youth is prized
above everything—there's so much road still in front of them, after all.

As many of us seek to reckon with our nation's original sin of racism,
others find such explorations tiresome and irrelevant, even threatening.
"That's all in the past," they say. "It doesn't have anything to do with me."
A Black president is a sign of a so-called post-racial future. We throw the
past over our shoulders, opting to revisit it only at safe, discrete, predeter-
mined times. Holidays. Anniversaries. Black History Month. (While many
applauded the addition of Juneteenth to the list of US holidays, commemorating the moment when news of emancipation finally came to Texas in
June of 1865, two and a half years after the Emancipation Proclamation,
some Black observers saw it as an attempt to affix a band-aid to a larger problem—window dressing rather than real economic or social justice.)

Such future orientation leaks into personal situations as well. *Aren't
you over this yet?* we ask people who continue to grieve a loss or process

a trauma longer than we think they "should." (If we're polite, we simply think it.) We are spiritually antsy, with little patience for examining the past. Better to cast it aside and hustle forward: another move in the liturgical dance of the Church of Moving On.

I'm as guilty of these moves as anyone. When I run races, I'm scarcely out of the finishers' chute before I'm thinking about the next one. (Ooh, can I beat my previous time?) In recent years I've taken to signing my emails with "Onward," though during the recent pandemic, I downshifted to "Steady on." At best, it's an encouragement to put one foot in front of the other. At worst, it's an injunction to keep going no matter what your body and heart are telling you, to strive at all costs.

A few years ago, I was bitten by a dog while on a wooded trail. The dog was never found, which means its vaccination status was unknown. I'm not a gambling woman when it comes to 100 percent fatal, 100 percent preventable diseases, so I submitted to the rabies prophylactic shots. (The series of four injections isn't as bad as you've heard, but it's no wine flight either.)

I remember talking to a mentor/friend of mine afterward. I laughed a little as I told the story, admitting how hard it had been, but I was quick to reflect on some deeper stuff as I moved forward with it. Churn and learn. Grist for the mill. Moral to the story. The preacher's special: three bullet points and a poem.

She said, "Hmm . . . It's good to reflect and learn and all that, but can we just pause for a minute and sit with the fact that you were assaulted by a dog on the running trail, which is one of your happy places, and now you have to do this inconvenient and awful thing?"

Oh. Yeah. That.

I'd tossed the past over my shoulder, before it was even really past.

That same week, Notre Dame Cathedral caught on fire, and people on the streets of Paris sang hymns on their knees as "Our Lady" burned. During that same time period, a number of African-American church buildings in Louisiana were set aflame in acts of domestic terrorism. The following Sunday was Easter. Did the saints in those places sing praise to the resurrection, and life out of death, and love being the last word, on Easter? Oh yes they did, because *that's what we do.*

But it's OK to take a minute, to look at the past right in front of our faces.

It's OK to sit with the grief for a while.

And it's OK to lament. It's OK to sing hymns on our knees, for a long time perhaps, before taking up the cries of "we will rebuild."

When we throw our past over our shoulders in our relentless Onward, I suspect hope suffers, because hope isn't always a growth enterprise. It requires us to be connected—to our deepest selves, our communities, our best purpose. In her work, sports psychologist Pippa Grange distinguishes between "winning shallow"—that is, winning to impress others—and "winning deep": "where you actually can feel the richness of your journey, you are attached to the joy and the struggle, you are attached to the mess, and it is generally done for reasons outside of yourself and the fulfillment of [your] egoic needs. It is done more from a soul level."[3]

Hope on the soul level is patient. Hope invites us to cradle the past, rest in the present, and dream a beautiful future—however long it takes.

Reflect

Do you find most of your energy in the past, present, or future of your life? How does this orientation move you deeper into hope, or take you away from it?

Practice

Ask a loved one to be an accountability partner for you, to listen for the times you are tempted to charge into the future rather than stay in the present.

THE FIRST PANEL of the cartoon features a woman saying to a man in a hospital bed, "This is all a part of God's plan."

The second panel features the stereotypical old man with long beard and robe, next to a white board:

Plan:
1. Make universe.
2. Give Steve a tumor.

Anyone who's spent any time among church folk will have heard the one about "God's plan." My flavor of Christianity is less prone to it than some, but we still rely on any number of snappy sentiments when we don't know what else to say.

Over the years I've developed a broad taxonomy of these statements:

Silver linings (these include the "at least" statements):
After a miscarriage: Well at least you know you can get pregnant.
At the death of a beloved spouse: You were married for such a long time; what a gift.

Vague assurances:
It's going to be OK.
Everything will turn out all right in the end.

Platitudes:

Grief is the price we pay for loving someone.

God never gives us more than we can handle.

Minimizing:

You'll get over it.

Others have it worse. (This one's often self-inflicted.)

These statements are almost always shared with the intent to provide care. Too often, though, they are foisted upon the person in grief for reasons that have more to do with the speaker than the bereaved. (As a wise friend quips, nothing says "I'm not listening to you" quite like reassurance.)

I will defend people's right to employ any of these for themselves, as a way of coping or making meaning. I'm worried, though, that this is what people say in times of suffering because they haven't been given anything better as an alternative. Is this the best we can do amid the reality of great pain?

We may be tempted to dismiss these statements as innocuous. Sure, they're a bit pithy, a pale substitute for true hope, but can they really do that much harm? Psychologist Susan David sees the impact of what she calls "toxic positivity" in her work. "Being positive has become a new form of moral correctness," she says. "People with cancer are automatically told to just stay positive. Women, to stop being so angry. And the list goes on. It's a tyranny. It's a tyranny of positivity. And it's cruel. Unkind. And ineffective. And we do it to ourselves, and we do it to others."[1]

One night, our daughter Caroline was tightly coiled into a ball of anxiety—in this case, a literal ball on the bed. I found myself arguing against a completely irrational-to-me series of thoughts. Of course, at the time I never would have called it arguing. I was "bearing witness to the truth," or "holding hope when others cannot," or whatever flowery language we use when justifying ourselves for trying to fix someone. But in that moment, my comfort was more important than my kid's reality.

It will surprise no one to learn that my assurances did nothing to calm my daughter. In fact, they seemed to make things worse. For every rejoinder, there was a counter. Finally I said quietly, "You know what . . . you're right. Sounds pretty bad."

In reality I was simply frustrated and fresh out of arguments. But wonder of wonders, through some mystery of grace, Caroline heard the quiet in my voice as understanding and not frustration, and visibly relaxed, relieved to be affirmed at last: *these thoughts are real, and they feel awful.* Only then could we work together to come to a different, more centered place. In time, the anxiety dissolved.

The encounter reminded me of the distinction between safe space and brave space. In her book *Brave Church,* Elizabeth Hagan discusses the importance of each space for authentic communication. "Safe spaces offer understanding, comfort, and belonging—gifts our souls crave," she writes. Safe spaces are especially vital for people whose experiences or identity are often threatened or viewed with suspicion, or in the case of people like Caroline, folks whose struggles are too often dismissed by our culture as being "all in their head."

Brave space, on the other hand, allows all parties to enter into the mystery that goes beyond answers and platitudes. We commit to muddling through together, whether it's a discussion about immigration policy or deep silence within a loved one's grief.[2]

Toxic positivity may feel safe, but as I discovered with my daughter, it's anything but. Authentic presence without answers, by contrast, is brave. And hopeful too.

Reflect

Make a list of some of the phrases you hear (or use!) when faced with challenging or painful circumstances. Whom do they serve? Do they bring you closer to hope or further from it?

Practice

Take a day or a week and do a "toxic positivity audit" of your social media and other communication sources. Where do you see unhelpful messages creeping in?

Hope Is Not Cause and Effect

~~~~~~

LIKE MANY PEOPLE during the pandemic, I tried my hand at sourdough bread. Armed with a foamy blob of starter I came to call Babs, I scoured the Internet until I found a recipe claiming to be both easy and foolproof. And it was. The bread never came out the same way twice—sometimes it was dense, sometimes light; sometimes it took a long time to bake and other times it puffed up quickly—but it was always bread and always edible. (Babs is currently languishing in a jar in the back of my fridge. Sorry, doll.)

I sometimes want hope to be like this: basically reliable, a straight line from cause to effect. If a cook knows their way around a kitchen and can follow instructions, they will generally yield a predictable result. The life of a cook is studded with occasional failures, and there's always more to learn, but the basic procedures are fixed. Assuming good ingredients, a trustworthy recipe, and competent skills, you will get an edible result. But I suspect a truly robust hope is more like gardening than baking.

Gardening is different from following a recipe, because so much is out of one's control. The quality of the soil. How hungry and determined the critters are. How much rain will come, or came last year. Heat waves. An early frost. As with cooking, gardeners learn and improve through trial and error. But in the end it's out of their hands.

Plus, the time horizon is much longer. Those little seeds nuzzle in the ground for a long time. There is waiting. There is watching.

My friend Derrick Weston works at the intersection of ecology, food, faith, and racial justice. He remembers working with a group of high school students to clean up and beautify an urban park that had fallen into decay. He decided to plant flowers with them:

> Planting flowers goes against a culture of death and violence. . . . The fact that they might get plucked up or crushed or that we'll have to do this all over again next year doesn't eliminate the value of planting flowers now. At the end of the day, I want to be the kind of person who would rather make a small, temporary gesture of goodness and beauty rather than add to the ugliness or do nothing at all. . . .
>
> Planting those flowers felt like an act of insurgency.[1]

An activist I know in the Bay Area who trains people in racial equity advocacy starts her trainings by telling people to get comfortable with a lack of closure. There is no linear progression, no list of bullet points, no specific benchmarks after which we're "finished."

This is bad news for those of us who are used to achieving measurable results. It's not that we shouldn't seek to be effective. But I'm realizing how often we substitute competence for hope. Hope acknowledges how much is beyond our control, and how easily cause and effect can slip out of gear.

A few days before he was killed, Harvey Milk made a recording to be shared in the event of his death. As the first openly gay person elected in the state of California, and a face of the LBGTQ+ movement, he knew his life was at risk. The video is a work of fierce defiance. It includes the bracing line, "All I ask is for the movement to continue, and if a bullet should enter my brain, let that bullet destroy every closet door."[2]

Milk joins a host of powerful civil rights figures in history whose final words catch in our throats with how prescient they turned out to be. Martin Luther King's final address is probably the most famous: "I've seen the promised land. I may not get there with you . . . [but] mine eyes have seen the glory of the coming of the Lord."[3] But there are others. Just a few weeks before his assassination, Fred Hampton, chair of the Illinois Black Panther Party, rhapsodized on what he called the beat of the people. "As long as you manifest the beat, we can never be stopped. . . . Don't worry about the Black Panther Party. As long as you keep the beat, we'll keep on going."[4]

I wonder sometimes how these leaders would assess where we are today. Have we made "enough" progress since their deaths? It's not frivolous to ask these questions—real people's lives are tied up in immense words like justice, equity, and peace. De-coupling hope from a linear cause and effect doesn't mean our efforts don't matter, that we shouldn't bring our best to the work of peace-building. And yes, perhaps these leaders would despair at how far we haven't come. But hope arcs beyond any of our own feeble lives and the results we produce—or don't. As Hampton said, "You can kill the revolutionary, but you cannot kill the revolution."

Hope, then, is an insurgent act, like flowers in an urban park.

Reflect

Reflect on hope as never finished. Is this a comforting or challenging thought?

Practice

Make a list of small, everyday acts of insurgency—like planting flowers—and commit to one each day for a week, or a month.

MANY A CHURCH CHOIR has sung these words, which have hung in living rooms and been embroidered on pillows:

> Where there is hatred,
> Let me sow love;
> Where there is injury, pardon;
> Where there is doubt, faith;
> Where there is despair, hope;
> Where there is darkness, light;
> Where there is sadness, joy;
> ... *Where there is despair, hope.*[1]

There's a gentleness and a conviction to this piece, attributed to St. Francis, a man who according to legend adored animals and lived lightly.

The kind of hope we see in the poem is echoed in much of Christian sacred text, which lifts up hope along with faith and love as the virtues that "abide." Paul assures us that "suffering produces endurance, and endurance produces character, and character produces hope, and hope does not disappoint us" (Rom. 5:3–5).

Hope is a major feature of our "secular scriptures" as well, appearing as a theme in countless books and movies: in the film *The Shawshank Redemption*, Andy Dufresne assures his cynical friend Red that "hope is a good thing, maybe the best of things, and no good thing ever dies."[2]

We're accustomed to seeing hope as an antidote to despair. But as much as I've been comforted by the binaries in St. Francis's words, I'm also suspicious of them. It's hard not to read the poem as the "bad" attribute being subsumed by the "good," of the former collapsing under the latter's positive weight. Doubt is no match for faith. Hatred's on the ropes as love delivers the knockout blow. Sadness may endure for the night, but joy comes in the morning.

Can't joy and mourning exist at the same time? As a parent who recently took a kid to college, and whose other two rudely insist on maturing and leaving the nest someday, I'm counting on it. The sadness makes the joy all the sweeter.

Having seen depression up close, I've realized the opposite of depression isn't happiness. The opposite of depression is *feeling*: feeling whole. Feeling alive, which can include joy and sadness; love and, yes, hatred. You can be alive and angry, even rageful. But you feel *something*. You are moved to do *something*.

Something similarly messy may be happening with despair and hope. Theologians such as Jurgen Moltmann have affirmed the two as opposites. But a lot depends on your social location. Ethicist Miguel de la Torre writes about the limits of hope, especially for marginalized communities. De la Torre writes on behalf of the people he meets in the desert, scrambling to cross the US-Mexican border, where five brown bodies die every four days. Many of them may profess and even feel hope. But others find alternate motivations, and for that group, says de la Torre, "The opposite of hope is not despair. The opposite of hope is desperation, because desperation propels me toward action. [Fear of] losing the little that I have keeps me quiet and docile. But when I have no hope, when I realize I have nothing to lose, that's when I'm the most dangerous"—that is, most willing to act to improve one's situation.[3]

For people like Moltmann—and, if I'm honest, for people like me—hell is synonymous with hopelessness; it's hard to imagine anything worse. But de la Torre argues, "Hell is where the vast majority of the world's oppressed currently live. And the question consistently ignored is: Who benefits from the creation of this hell?"[4]

After Jacob Blake was shot by police in Kenosha, Wisconsin, author and speaker Austin Channing Brown tweeted, "I get asked about hope a lot when talking about race in America. White folks usually mean 'are you optimistic.' But Black folks connect hope to duty, legacy, the good fight. Kenosha is why."[5] For Brown, and for de la Torre, hope—if it's even required or relevant at all—is connected with action, not as an antidote or corrective to despair but fueled by it, for its own sake. As de la Torre says, it's "an act of courage to embrace reality, and to act even when the odds are in favor of defeat." Perhaps despair and hope aren't opposites at all; perhaps they beat within the same yearning human heart.

The mythical nation of Wakanda stands at this interplay between despair and hope in the Black Panther stories, particularly the 2018 film of the same name. Wakanda is technologically advanced and hidden, which allows the country to remain disconnected from the plight of Black people around the world. Over time, T'Challa (who is both king and Black Panther) comes to realize that Wakandans cannot stay sequestered and protected from the rest of the world. They must enter the fray, working for justice and the flourishing of their people around the world.

In a number of Marvel films, T'Challa rallies his Wakandan troops with the cry of "Yibambe!" which is a Xhosa word meaning "be strong" or "hold fast."[6] I love that, at pivotal moments of battle, the war cry isn't "Charge!" or "Take no prisoners!" or "Show no mercy!" or some other swaggering Rambo-inflected line. It is simply, *Be strong. Hold the line. Stand with courage.* Focus on the task, regardless of how we "feel." When we hold the line, when we stand with courage, we may still experience despair or even desperation. But the standing is itself a hopeful act, and the best kind of hope: hope on its own terms.

Reflect

React to the idea of hope and despair dwelling together, rather than one canceling the other.

Practice

Try on Austin Channing Brown's idea of hope as connected to "duty, legacy, and the good fight." How does this notion move you to live your life differently?

I WAS DRIVING with two of my kids through the rural Midwest when we ran across a church sign:

Look to eternity when the present is collapsing around you.

I found myself wondering what kind of "collapsing" was occurring in that community that was causing the most alarm (small-town life? economic opportunity? family values? declining church membership?) when one of the kids broke into my thoughts: "What if there is no eternity?" The other nodded his approval.

I don't blame my skeptical teens for being cynical. As the generation that will need to clean up the environmental mess we've made, and the first generation in our nation's history projected to fare worse economically than their parents, they're entitled to be salty when they see signs like that. (How about doing something *about* the collapse?)

I remembered a conversation decades before with a college friend about my recent return to religion. After many years of viewing faith with scorn, I was as surprised as anyone to meet and fall in love with a Presbyterian preacher's kid and to realize his particular slice of Christianity loved God with the mind, revered science, and wasn't interested in damning people to hell so much as helping the world be the kind of place Jesus taught it could be.

I was still new at this faith stuff, though, and found it hard to explain the appeal to my thoroughly secular friend. "I think I get it," he said. "That need for solace."

Solace? I thought. *No, no! That's not it at all!*

Solace—consolation in times of sadness—is one of the fruits of religion. And why not? Life is difficult for countless reasons. It's comforting to believe that this nasty, brutish, and short existence is not the end of the line; that when the world is collapsing, there's another one waiting for us. In this way, solace and hope are connected, binary stars orbiting around one another.

"Solace" is an old-fashioned word. According to Google Books, its use in print was in steady decline since the 1870s—until 1980, when its popularity began to climb sharply, more sharply than other churchy words like "grace" and "mercy." By 2019 it was popping up as often as it had in 1883.

Why? Who can say? Perhaps the rise of "solace" reflects the sense that the world is coming ever so dramatically unspooled. It's all a mess, so we'll settle for comfort in the sweet by and by. Hope seems too far away in its orbit, so we train our telescopes on solace instead. *Look to eternity when the present is collapsing.*

There's a quote from actress and comedian Gilda Radner emblazoned on a wall in the Second City Training Center in Chicago: "Life is about not knowing what's going to happen next—delicious ambiguity." It's a poignant line, especially from an entertainer who died at forty-two after an excruciating battle with ovarian cancer. Sometimes the ambiguity isn't delicious; sometimes it's downright painful, and there's not much solace to be found in it.

Miguel de la Torre, in his work around hopelessness, evokes the image of Holy Saturday—that time after Jesus's crucifixion but before the resurrection, before the glorious surprise ending of the story. "I have chosen to stand in radical solidarity with the oppressed of the world who live in Holy Saturday," he says. "Not knowing if there even is a resurrection on Sunday is to lose control of time and history and be in the moment of anxiety and not knowing."[1] *Screw your solace,* he seems to be saying.

But those of us with faith in the end of the story, those of us who affirm the resurrection, aren't off the hook from that radical presence and shared unknowing. The resurrection is not an answer, but a new set of questions: How will we now live? What does the resurrection call forth from us? Those are hope questions, and solace is a poor substitute.

That's what I would have told my college friend, if I'd had the words. I'm not here for warm milk and a bedtime story, as reassuring as those things are sometimes.

A while later, my kids and I saw a second sign in front of a different church, one that suited us better and expressed what true hope might look like if we look beyond mere solace:

> If you've been blessed with good fortune, build a bigger table, not a higher fence.

Reflect

Explore the relationship between solace and hope. How are they related for you? Do you find yourself relying on one over the other?

Practice

Practice "delicious ambiguity." When you find yourself striving to understand or explain, resist the temptation.

Hope Is Not Future-Proofing

~~~~~~

SOME TIME AGO, I spoke at a congregation not far from my home in the suburbs of DC, sharing one of my favorite topics, which is improvisation and the spiritual life. How do we respond when things don't go according to plan? (As we addressed earlier, is there even such a thing as a cosmic "plan"?) What resources do we draw on when we need to find our way without a map? How does faith help us live with courage in times of calamitous change?

This particular church is populated with what I call "masters of the universe": government officials, heads of NGOs, think tank wonks, and so forth. One of them folded his arms and said, "Improv is all well and good when the unexpected happens, but what we really need is to get better at eliminating the need to improvise at all. I mean, in an ideal world, we'd know what was going to happen. We'd anticipate all the possible outcomes and be able to plan for them all."

For all I know, this gentleman works for one of DC's secretive three-letter agencies with the immense task of keeping millions of people safe, and who depends on copious high-quality intelligence to do so. (These are the people who, when you ask what they do for a living, say they work for "the government.") I want him to have every bit of intel he needs. Still, the conversation up to that point had centered around more quotidian, personal matters: navigating a health diagnosis, for example, or improvising amid career changes and retirement. As such, it was hard for me to keep a poker face. Knowing *all* possible outcomes? Even the United

States Marine Corps, not known for flying by the seat of their perfectly pressed pants, embraces the phrase "improvise, adapt, and overcome" as one of its many slogans.

I later learned there's a word for what the man was proposing, which is "future-proofing": anticipating what's to come and minimizing the impact of the shocks and stresses those events will bring. I asked my husband if it was a word people actually used in business, and he confirmed with an example: "We've built the phone's operating system with support for 5G already, so it's future-proof." (It will be fun to read this book in a few years' time and reflect on how obsolete that supposedly future-proof example is.)

I get it. Organizations need a sense of what's coming so they're not blown about by every shift, dip, or trend. As much as I love improv as a life skill, there are certain benefits to at least some long-range planning. But most of us are pretty change averse. Given the choice, we'll cling to certainties and wrestle for control any way we can get it. Against the backdrop of human nature, future-proofing doesn't seem like sound organizational practice. It feels like a jargony hedge against the cataclysmic anxiety that has run rampant at every level in recent years.

Which brings me back to the masters of the universe. It's not that we should careen headlong into the future with no preparation. I just find the idea that we would anticipate every hypothetical, that there would be no surprises whatsoever, utterly exhausting. Let's set aside whether it would ever be possible to predict every single potential outcome and have all possible game plans ready to go. Is it, in fact, "ideal" to always know what's going to happen? I often joke that I like my backup plans to have backup plans, but I'm not on board with airtight preparedness either.

I suspect that such a closed system provides no room for hope. In fact, it eliminates the whole need for it. I admire the effort to prepare and plan, but in addition to orienting us, hope also keeps us the right size. If we have it all figured out, if the future is full of certainties we've sketched out on our whiteboards, we don't require hope anymore.

More than looking into the crystal ball and identifying emerging trends, I think the real future-proofing is to lean into hope: to clarify our values and build skills to survive the onslaught of change. The World Economic Forum recently defined the most important job skills for the coming decade. Topping the list? Complex problem solving, critical thinking, creativity, people management, and emotional intelligence.[1]

Human-centered pursuits, not foregone conclusions. That's how hope can break in.

Reflect

React to the idea of future-proofing. How is the concept useful? Where does it fall short?

Practice

Try on the Marine Corps slogan "Improvise, adapt, overcome" with a particularly challenging situation. What do you notice when you do?

2

What Hope Is

We've talked about what hope *isn't*. But what *is* it?

Having cleared out some of the clutter in section 1, it's time to invest in ideas of hope that are sturdier than what we're leaving behind. In this section, we explore some nuances and possibilities of what hope might be. Here we find not definitions but excursions: detours and discoveries, parables and promises.

As you read, consider: Where are you being invited next? Where do you sense resistance? What might that resistance be telling you?

—

~~~~~~

MENTAL HEALTH ISSUES often spring up when the old ways of surviving no longer work. Starting in middle school, my kid experienced brutal performance anxiety and school anxiety, and coped by buckling down, working harder, and pushing ever greater perfection. These strategies "worked" for a time, until they no longer did, resulting in an emotional reckoning that took more than a year to sort itself out. Now our child is better: kinder, more self-forgiving, less performance oriented, less perfectionistic. I like to say, "Caroline, you blasted through stuff in eighteen months that I've been dealing with in dribs and drabs for thirty years."

But depression and anxiety don't disappear overnight. They can lie dormant and come out to wreak havoc at unexpected times. We dealt with these demons during the COVID crisis, when Caroline was ready to road-test new skills and attitude, only to hurtle into a pandemic along with the rest of the world. This meant online school, no extracurriculars, and an altered prom—though the matching masks along with color-coordinated gowns and cummerbunds were both sweet and poignant.

Like many parents, Robert and I decided that the curriculum of getting through a global pandemic was more important than the particulars of linear algebra or Mary Shelley's *Frankenstein*. My kids—and our whole family—muddled through, powered by mantras like "world's okayest" and "this doesn't matter" (because most of it didn't). But there were tears at times. After an especially stressful day, Caroline asked this wrenching question: "What if I can't handle college? What if I start to spiral again, like I did in high school?"

What would you say to this, if it were your kid?

Here's where my mind went first: *Oh, you won't. You've learned so much. You're on medication that's helping you manage really well. College is going to be completely different. And you won't be in a freaking pandemic . . . hopefully?*

I certainly reassured Caroline with messages like this from time to time. I would downshift to optimism, offering some kind of prediction about the future. And my daughter would dutifully nod—"yeah that's true"—and *I* would feel better.

But this time, for whatever reason, I paused for a long time and then I said, "Well, what *if* you start to spiral?"

The responses were immediate and heartbreaking.

I'll flunk out.

I'll have to leave college.

I won't graduate.

I'll never find a job and will live at home forever.

I'll be a failure.

I interrupted. "Wait a minute. No, that's not what I meant. I mean, what if that happens? Literally. What will you do? What will you do first? What will you do next?"

The answers came a little slower, but they came.

"I will ask for help. I will talk to my professors. I will schedule a therapy appointment. I will speak to my psychiatrist. I will practice self-care."

There it is.

To be clear, Caroline's blurted-out fears could come to pass. Every single one of them could. Depression is a persistent SOB. But none of those worries will inspire purposeful action. Fear rarely does. But knowing what we can't control and acting on what we can? That's hope in the flesh.

One of my heroes, Mitri Raheb, is a Lutheran pastor in Bethlehem— yes, *that* Bethlehem—and president of the Dar Al-Kalima University College of Arts and Culture. His entire life since the age of five has taken place under occupation. A self-described "prisoner of hope," Raheb could have left the region, as so many Palestinian Christians have. Instead he faithfully labors on behalf of his people and his homeland, imagining a liberated future for Palestine.

This labor comes at a cost. He recalls giving up a high school graduation party after a classmate was imprisoned following a peaceful protest. He and his wife never had a wedding reception when they married in 1989. A year later, his young family along with others in the region faced the threat of poisonous gas attacks from Saddam Hussein. "It's hard to start over so many times," Raheb says. "Occupation touches lives in horrible ways."[1]

And yet his motto—his statement of faith—is "hope is what we do." I love the double meaning: hope is "what we do" in the sense of the business we're in, like "writing and coaching is what I do." But even deeper is this: Hope is wrapped up in what we make real. Hope isn't what we think. Hope isn't what we feel. Hope isn't even what we imagine is possible. Hope is what we *do* in the face of suffering, pain, and injustice. Hope is what we do in the face of depression's dull weight or grief's harsh sting. Hope is what we do.

Reflect

Reflect on hope as a series of actions rather than a feeling.

Practice

Pick an issue or situation that feels overwhelming and intractable. Do one tiny thing in response. What do you notice afterward?

~~~~~~

IN THE SUMMER OF 2021, the cicadas returned. Brood X, to be exact, which emerges from the ground every seventeen years to eat, mate, die— and, in the case of the males, make noise. The drone powered up in early spring and reached a nerve-scrambling pitch by May and June. I likened it to the UFO sound effect in a cheap 1950s movie. It seemed almost mechanical, a tinny vibrato, and for weeks on end it did not stop.

Here in the Mid-Atlantic, we cheered the novelty—for a while. Then the fatigue set in. A friend required noise-canceling headphones just to hear herself think. In some areas, they were louder than a lawn mower. Dogs ate them and vomited the remains onto couches. Cicadas are un- gainly things, and it seems improbable that they'd be able to fly, but they do, bumbling their way into people, grabbing on to clothes, getting tan- gled in hair. They're homely, comical little creatures, with beady red eyes, ugly black bodies, and that year, a white fungus that infected their butts, increasing their mating prowess and producing a psychedelic effect.[1] (At least someone was having fun during the pandemic.)

There's something both comforting and implausible about their life cycle. Seventeen years! They come like clockwork, yet on such a pecu- liar timeline. Seventeen is a prime number, for heaven's sake. It's as if they're thumbing their nose at humanity's silly, regimented base-ten numbering system.

The last time they visited, Caroline was a year old. I was too im- mersed in keeping my head above water to take much note of these sea-

sonal visitors, except that when the UFO landed in 2021, I remembered
the sound. One memory remains of the 2004 season, though. I'd asked
a church group to share some holy moments in their lives, and one older
woman said, "Holy are the cicadas, that will return when your daughter
and my grandson graduate high school." Such an otherworldly occur-
rence didn't seem possible at the time.

This latest arrival took on a different meaning, influenced by the
world in 2021. I was glad when they showed up. Our planet is roiling,
and it's not hard to imagine a time, seventeen or thirty-four or fifty-one
years from now, when the expected emergence doesn't happen. Or the
brood becomes so prolific as to be downright biblical, adding insult to
the injury of an ever-escalating climate crisis.

The other thing I noticed that year, the COVID year, is that ubiquitous cicadas meant ubiquitous, well, death. Their carcasses dotted the
sidewalks. By the end of the season, their carcasses *covered* the sidewalks.
They were everywhere—flattened on the path, intact but motionless on
the grass, piled up beside tree trunks. Billions of cicadas meant billions
of dead cicadas. They'd mated, yes, fulfilling their evolutionary mandate,
but not where I could see; what I witnessed was their abundant, uncere-
monious end. I thought of the nature documentaries I watched with my
son: the programs' painstaking balance between trumpeting animals'
victories (outwitting the predator, rebuilding the destroyed nest) and
honestly conveying how perilous their lives are, in no small part because
of humans. Each female cicada lays four hundred to six hundred eggs,
but only a fraction of these make it to adulthood. I'm not eager for more,
but that's brutal math.

As a child, I had an LP record that told various folk tales. Years later,
only one stays with me: the story of Pandora, who opens a forbidden
box and lets loose all manner of pestilence, despair, cruelty, and evil into
the world. But there's one little entity at the bottom of the box that also
escapes, and that is Hope.

It's as decent a parable as any to describe the human condition, and
the proportions certainly seem right. If hope outweighed suffering, we
wouldn't really need it—it would simply be the predictable order of

things for good always to prevail. Instead, it seems hope is destined to be the underdog.

It's a comfort to know that the cicadas fulfilled their reproductive destiny before they were eaten, got squished, or succumbed to butt fungus. We won't know for another seventeen years just how prolific the mating season was, whether pint-sized Hope has smiled upon their frantic efforts. In the meantime, I am left with images of carnage.

What rings false about Pandora's parable, though, is the instantaneous act of unleashing it all. Despair and cruelty proliferate, not thanks to one catastrophic unboxing but a thousand small decisions, compromises, dehumanizations. And similarly, hope is not a singular entity but a thousand silvery threads. Small threads, though, amid a lot of gloomy pain.

I always pictured Hope in Pandora's story as a petite, sprite-like figure, fragile yet plucky. Upon reflection, I may have conflated the final escapee from the box with the young girl who dared to open it. In my mind's eye, Hope looked like Pandora herself. And maybe that, too, is the point. Hope looks like all of us. We, who have unleashed so much misery, are also the bearers of a small bit of antidote. Sometimes, if I'm honest, it doesn't feel like enough. The destruction piles up, until it's all I'm able to see.

Reflect

Is hope necessary in order to move forward? Why or why not?

Practice

Imagine you don't feel hope, or imagine hope is in short supply. (For some of us, this won't be hard.) What if you gave up on trying to scrape together "enough" hope? Where would you turn instead in order to persevere?

~~~~~~

ONE OF THE INTERNET's greatest hits for our family is a video of an Oreo separator machine. Melding charm with precision, the invention uses an arm to drop each cookie in place, a hatchet to separate the two sides, and a CNC router table to scrape off the creme. We marvel at the creativity of the design and the "just because you can" exuberance of the project, even as we shake our heads at the fact that the designer David Neevel harvests the *cookies* for eating and discards the *filling*. (Heresy.)

This type of machine is known as a Rube Goldberg device, a contraption that performs some (usually simple) function using a series of whimsical chain reactions. There are tons of examples online, but it's easy to replicate with a group of people, using an improv game called, simply, Machine. A person steps to the front and does a simple repetitive motion. Bonus points if they make a sound to go with it. The next person steps up and does a second motion and sound, different from the first but somehow connected to it. Play continues until all have joined the machine. It matters not if the gadget actually "accomplishes" something concrete. Its purpose has been fulfilled: to knit the group together and build community.

A good story is a kind of chain-reaction device. X leads to Y leads to Z. Scripture has a ton of these stories, in which seemingly unrelated circumstances conspire to bring about a wondrous outcome, a result that often feels both improbable and inevitable.

Here's my favorite Rube Goldberg story from the Hebrew Bible: a famine decimates the land, leading to the death of a woman's two grown sons. The widow of one son, moved by loving-kindness, makes the daring decision to stay with her mother-in-law, despite not being obligated by blood or custom to do so. Desperate for food, they encounter a man who permits gleaning of his field. Mother-in-law sees an opening, one thing leads to another, and the man and her daughter-in-law marry. That daring, kind woman has a son, who has a son, who has a son, a boy named David, who will come to be the most beloved of Israel's kings. Many generations later, another child will be born whose life exemplifies the daring and loving-kindness of his foremother, one of the few women mentioned by name in his genealogy. The child, of course, is Jesus. And so the woman, Ruth, who knew the trauma of loss, the terror of drought, and the spasms of hunger, is connected by family and history to the One who would bind up the brokenhearted and be called living water and the bread of life.

A common feature of Rube Goldberg devices is that they do simple things in a complicated way. If God wanted to, God could have cut out a lot of that story, with its attendant challenges and miseries, and skipped right to the redemptive end. In fact, many understandably use the circuitous route as evidence that the whole God thing is a sham. I'm sympathetic.

I myself am compelled by the idea of the Spirit of Life and Love and Yes being in the mess with us, partnering with us in every excruciating one of these beautiful and terrible chain reactions. A church I know has had a ministry for and with the day laborers in their community for years, which is a story all its own. Day laborers work hand to mouth without the benefit of insurance, and one of these men was diagnosed with cataracts. The church found out his plight and scraped together some discretionary funds to help him, but it wasn't quite enough. Another church raised a bit of money too, but it wasn't quite enough. Together, though, it was enough, along with an offer of rides to and from the surgery. Now the man, named Jesús, can see, and he can work, and he can call together a bunch of his fellow day laborers for a cleanup effort in a local neighborhood, making the community more comfortable and livable, which is exactly what he did. X leads to Y leads to Z.

Such Rube Goldberg contraptions are beautiful to me as conveyor belts of hope, but they're fragile. These intricate machines depend on everything going right. What if Ruth had gone home? What if only one church had found the money to help Jesús?

Part of the Jewish Passover Seder is to recount the story of God bringing the people out of slavery and into freedom. There's a song that names these moves, with a refrain of *dayenu*, meaning "it would have been enough."

> Had God brought us out of Egypt, only brought us out of
> Egypt . . . it would have been enough.
> Had God given us the Torah, only given us the Torah . . .
> it would have been enough.
> Had God given us the Sabbath, only given us the Sabbath . . .
> it would have been enough.

Perhaps *dayenu* provides a little lubricant when the machine gets creaky. If Ruth's only act had been to stay by Naomi's side, being her companion until old age claimed them both, *dayenu*. If the congregation's only act had been to do everything it could to support Jesús and stand with him, even if the total fell short, *dayenu*.

Dayenu doesn't permit us to take the short view on justice and wholeness, to throw up our hands and say, "Oh well, we tried." What it does is invite us to see the grace in each link of the story, to celebrate that whatever else happened, for one miraculous moment, someone chose hope.

But *dayenu*—"enough"—also bears a marvelous secret: if we truly act as if we are enough—if we believe our X or Y or Z is sufficient to the task—our individual offerings, put together, can often accomplish more than we imagine is possible.

Reflect

"I myself am compelled by the idea of the Spirit of Life and Love and Yes being in the mess with us, partnering with us in every excruciating one of these beautiful and terrible chain reactions." React to this statement.

Practice

Reflect on the chain reactions in your life—the small actions and shifts that brought you to where you are. Who made a difference? Share with them the impact they had.

WITH A BIRTHDAY on the first of January, I can never resist approaching the new year as a chance to take stock. Sometimes I'll choose a word for the coming year, some attribute or wisdom to guide me in the months to come. On a whim, at the beginning of 2020 I chose "serenity."

Given what befell the entire world by March of that year, focusing on serenity turned out to be one of the best practices I ever tumbled into.

Serenity, according to the famous prayer, comes through accepting the things we can't change and changing the things we can. The year 2020 gave me a lot of opportunities to practice making that distinction, though I suspect it's the work of my lifetime, COVID or no COVID.

I recently had the honor of bearing witness as a new friend shared her journey with cancer and her current remission. She offered her story with all the intimacy of a fireside chat, despite taking place on Zoom.

At the moment of the diagnosis, including a grim prognosis, my friend experienced a profound, paradoxical sense of both acceptance and nonacceptance. In a flash, she had to accept: any semblance of control and mastery over her life was gone, and whether it ever returned was beyond her. She was stepping into the unknown. At the same time, she moved into nonacceptance. If she was not in control, then maybe nobody else was either, including her doctors with their so-called certainties. Even with their medical training and expertise (which she trusted and relied upon), she knew that the math of prognosis is based on odds and percentages. She felt equally invested in both sides of the paradox, both acceptance and nonacceptance, and that helped her move forward.

Her acceptance yielded an equanimity that buoys her to this day, while the nonacceptance allowed her to be defiant, hopeful, even playful. She remembers well when a doctor said, "You probably have two years left." With a start, she said, "Two years from when? Right this minute? If I had my appointment a month from now, would you have said two years then as well? How about if the two years starts two years from now, can I do that?"

When we feel we have no options, the clarity of the serenity prayer, of acceptance and nonacceptance, allows us to choose . . . something. To choose to look for hope. To choose not to give up. To choose to make the most of a bad situation. To choose to allow ourselves to be heartbroken. To choose to do what's ours to do and leave the outcome to someone or something else, or fate, or God.

Besides being a paradox, acceptance and nonacceptance become cyclical. Acceptance breeds nonacceptance: when we acknowledge how out of control we are, we have the capacity to give our whole hearts to the places where we need to fight back. And nonacceptance breeds acceptance. By giving something our all, it engenders peace to let go of outcome and trust we could have done no more.

What finally helped our daughter recover from debilitating anxiety and depression was exposure therapy—structured exercises designed to increase a person's tolerance for the stressful experience. During this therapeutic experience, Caroline and other teens struggling with school anxiety learned coping skills and self-regulation techniques. They practiced encountering the stressful situation in small doses, then slightly bigger ones, and over time their resilience grew.

Exposure therapy begins with a base of acceptance: acceptance that people are valuable and worth feeling better, and acceptance that the path forward is not going to be easy; it will take work.

But the beauty of exposure therapy is in its nonacceptance, its refusal to accept life as fixed and unchanging. From a place of positive self-regard, we can love ourselves enough to stretch into a new way of being.

Reflect

Make a list of what you can and can't accept. How does acceptance lead you into hope? How does nonacceptance?

Practice

Post the serenity prayer somewhere you can see it. Make it a regular part of your day. (This prayer can be adapted as a more general affirmation if "God language" is not native to you.)

Hope Is Either On or Off

In my work coaching leaders, I've noticed a couple themes that often emerge simultaneously.

First, many people are perpetually flirting with burnout—too much to do, high levels of turmoil, not enough clarity, paltry self-care.

At the same time, many people (often the same ones as above) feel they aren't doing enough, usually because they're grading themselves on a curve of what they see from others, which is always distorted. And we're not even grading ourselves against particular individuals: we take every snippet from social media and elsewhere and amalgamate them into a single superhero who is doing everything right. A perfectly productive person who somehow has plenty of time for meditative mornings sipping coffee. An effortless parent who's also crushing it at work, tending a prolific garden, volunteering at the food pantry, managing a sparkling home, and pursuing a burgeoning side hustle on Etsy. We are judging ourselves against a construct, a composite.

Some time ago a running friend introduced me to the term *pass-fail running*, and I loved it instantly. When you're in a long training cycle and building up to a race, a coach or training plan may schedule a variety of workouts: long runs, short easy sessions, speedwork, hill repeats, and so on. Each of these workouts serves a particular physiological purpose, and together they get you ready for your event. But good races are not built on the excellence we bring to this training. Good races are built on

49

consistency. And consistency, oddly enough, means getting out there and doing *something*, even if the "something" wasn't on the plan.

When we're working at diminished capacity due to uncertainty, grief, and financial realities—*or* we're working at *over*capacity because our responsibilities are piled on top of one another—excellence is a dead end. Consistency, paradoxically, gives us options, because it sets up a manageable choice: do nothing, with "perfection," or do something—*anything*—as best you can in that moment.

Imagine a runner with a track workout scheduled for Tuesday, but Tuesday comes and she's feeling tired.

If *excellence* is her standard, she'll skip the track because she knows there's no way she'll hit her pace targets.

If *consistency* is her standard, she'll put on her workout clothes and run the neighborhood instead. Or walk with a friend. Or do ten minutes of stretching.

Pass-fail effort. It's the way of Yoda: do or do not; there is no try.

Does consistency mean we never take a day off? Of course not—rest is vital to good running and good human-ing. What it means is that the imperfect thing we did means everything, and the perfect thing we left undone serves no one. In a world of limited capacity and best-laid plans, doing what little we can is the actual superhero move.

Years ago, a new community-organizing effort brought together congregations throughout Northern Virginia to agitate with elected leaders for the sake of the underserved in the region. The nascent group knew it wanted to work in health care and explored a number of options and initiatives. Community organizing is practical and tactical. Rather than advocate for something big and out of reach, they wanted their first initiative to succeed, giving them momentum on which to build. Where they ultimately found their first success was in dental care—specifically, reallocation of county funds to hire a dentist to serve low-income populations in the western part of the county.

It may not seem like much in comparison to the looming giant that is health-care access for people in poverty. I hope nobody suggests as much to my friend Becca Messman, a pastor who worked on the effort. She got involved after hearing about a man in the community who extracted four of his own molars because he lacked the money to pay for dental care. Their consistency made a difference to real people, people like him.

People sometimes talk about being low on hope, or worry that hope is in too-short supply. I propose we consider hope as a binary phenomenon, a pass-fail condition. As the old saying goes, nobody's "a little bit pregnant." Maybe hope works the same way. When Pandora threw open that box, all manner of calamity escaped, with Hope a wispy afterthought. But the moral of the story is, even that much hope is adequate. My hope may not be *excellent*, but it's imperfectly, sloppily *consistent*.

In this way, hope can be the small candle flame that illumines a dark room. Often there isn't much difference between one candle and ten— it's the first one that makes the biggest impact. Perhaps Rabbi Adam Kligfeld has this in mind when he reflects on the meaning of Hanukkah, the Jewish holiday commemorating an ancient miracle that kept the lamp oil flowing for eight days. Kligfeld suggests that the real miracle isn't that the lamps never ran dry; the real miracle is that someone had enough hope to light them at all.[1]

Reflect

Reflect on the idea that consistency is more important than excellence.

Practice

For the next week, pursue as much as you can in a pass-fail way. Have a friend help you be accountable. See what you notice.

~~~~~~

IN AN EFFORT to expand our son's interests beyond science fiction books and video games, we subscribed him to a service that sends a monthly kit to be put together. Our favorite so far has been a lockbox—a wooden box with a key and lock that, when turned, allows a multi-paneled door to slide open in a cute and elegant way.

The first step was putting the lock together. James followed the instructions, with me sitting nearby primarily for company. A few times he needed some extra hands to hold the head of a screw in place so it would tighten properly.

The lock has a series of moving parts that go up and down depending on whether they are triggered by the key. As we tested it out, we realized that we'd fastened some of the pieces too tightly to move easily. Others weren't tight enough.

What we'd stumbled into was the difference between loose and tight tolerance, which Adam Savage explores in his book *Every Tool's a Hammer: Life Is What You Make It.*

When machines are assembled, they're put together with various levels of tolerance, which is broadly defined as the precision with which the pieces match one another—whether they fit tightly or loosely together. The appropriate level of tolerance depends on the machine, its purpose and use.

Machines with loose tolerance have a lot of give in them. I picture Mater, the lovable tow truck in the *Cars* animated movies. Mater could generously be called a bucket of bolts, but he doesn't *need* a tight tolerance to be a good tow truck; in fact, loose-tolerance machines are often assembled as such so they can be repaired easily and handle lots of wear and tear in the meantime. Given how often we see Han Solo and Chewbacca tinkering with the Millennium Falcon, I suspect the so-called hunk of junk to have loose tolerance. But as Han reminds us, "She's got it where it counts."

Sports cars, on the other hand, are ultra-precise, with measurements down to the ten-thousandth of an inch.[1] If the Falcon is loose, the imperial star destroyers are tight. Tight tolerance is reserved for the highest-performing equipment. Every machine is subject to vibration, says Savage. Loose-tolerance machines are built to absorb it; tight-tolerance ones are built to minimize it or channel it into the engine's performance.

Neither loose nor tight tolerance is better than the other; these are value-neutral distinctions. Which one we choose depends on the purpose of the machine and what we expect from it. Both have strengths and weaknesses, though. Loose-tolerance machines work fine so long as they operate within their expected parameters. If they run too fast or too long without service, they will fall apart. But they can also handle lots more "slop," which is what Savage calls the dirt and junk that can get inside the inner workings.

Savage is writing about life as well as machinery. There's a cost to putting our lives together with too little tolerance, too little "give." This comes up often when I coach clients who are exhausted from the effort of tightening down so many bolts. Often they'd like to keep things a little looser, a little more flexible and Mater-like, but they work within systems that expect precision at all costs. This is especially true for women and people of color, whom society typically affords less margin of error.

In a previous section, we explored how hope is decoupled from cause and effect. As such, I believe hope tends more toward loose tolerance than tight. Hope expects things to be chaotic and loosens the screws, ever so slightly, in the name of keeping the apparatus together.

Loose tolerance requires us to relinquish some control, which is always easier said than done. My friend Tim Hughes Williams is a fellow pastor and student of improv comedy. He says, "What I learned from improv is that if you are a good performer, you can *act* like you are yes-anding but still feel very in control of the situation. But improv just doesn't work [that way] . . . you're ruining it if you're doing that. You're still managing it. You're aggressively managing it in the most 'casual' way possible."

In other words, are we *really* going with the flow, or are we just acting like it? Am I *really* a hopeful person, or am I acting hopeful while resting in my own proficiency?

A tweet by Jordan Lancaster says this:

Boomers: I heard she went to [looks around nervously] [whispers] ~therapy~

Millennials/Gen Z: LMAOOOO YALL GUESS WHAT MY THERAPIST TOLD ME TODAY[2]

Yes, I know plenty of Boomers who go to therapy. (And once again, my own Generation X is invisible.) But I'm heartened when I see how openly my kids' generation talks about mental health, how openly they accept racial diversity, LGBTQ diversity, religious diversity, and the like. That's loose tolerance. In his book, Savage extols the benefits and joys of what he calls mistake tolerance: the willingness to be kind to ourselves when our efforts fall short, and to try again and again.[3]

What he's describing is grace. And hope is rigid and false without it.

Reflect

Consider the areas of your life that have tight tolerance and loose tolerance. Have you calibrated things in a life-giving way? Are shifts necessary?

Practice

At the end of each day, reflect on your day with an abundance of kindness, giving yourself grace for the things left undone. (A friend once said she began each day with the prayer "Whatever," and ended the day with "Oh well." Try it.)

Hope Is the Long View

~~~~~~

WHEN CAROLINE STARTED struggling, doctors would ask, "Is there a history of depression in the family?" I never quite knew how to answer. No . . . but yes? There were no direct analogs to what my kid was enduring. But the family tree was studded with alcoholism and drug use. I would relay this to the doctor, shrug, and say, "I guess they were self-medicating for something, right?" Random memories of my extended family came unbidden: the faded photographs of uncles jokingly putting a beer can next to a toddler's lips. The framed prints of twelve-step slogans hanging in front hallways. The sobriety birthdays. The relapses, the new birthdays. The whispered stories of abuse.

I heard a well-known author recently say he had a happy childhood but wasn't a happy child. His struggles are his own, but I think a lot of us can relate to a childhood that seemed pretty normal until we cock our heads and go, *oh wait, that was a little off.* My family lived in an idyllic Houston neighborhood where nobody seemed to particularly struggle. I remember a good friend coming for a sleepover the night her father entered the hospital. My parents asked her what was wrong with him and she said quietly, "Bronchitis." The next day my dad, a decade sober at that point, said, "He's detoxing." I was stunned. "What?" He went on. "Did you see the way she looked down at her plate when she said it—she was coached to say that. To lie." I hadn't seen it. It's like his own recovery had become a superpower—X-ray vision, cutting right through the bull.

I still didn't believe it until I confronted my friend at school. But it was true. I can still picture us in a crowded middle-school stairwell, realizing we had this thing in common: an alcoholic father. We tried to speak loud enough to be heard over the echoing din of students, but not so loud that we could be heard by the people pouring past. Although how many of them had similar issues lurking in their own "perfect" households?

My father's older brother recently passed away. We weren't close— I have vague memories from childhood of a former Marine who was both goofy and a bit strange. I followed the updates from my cousin with interest and sadness—his nephew, not his son (my uncle never had kids). He'd suffered a fall, but they couldn't do an MRI until he had detoxed, and the process was horrible and brutal. His body essentially shut down. Almost two decades after my own father's sudden death, I gave thanks once again for his sobriety.

I balk sometimes at how hard the emotional work is to get and be healthy. (I also never met a self-improvement job that I didn't throw myself into; moderating that impulse is emotional work all its own.) My therapist always reminds me that everything we do is generation-level work. We heal and grow; we get a little bit better so that our kids will have it a little bit easier. She tells me this because I will do for my own kids what I will not do for myself. But she also tells me this because the work necessitates patience.

My own father could be a real pain in the butt. We had blistering conflicts after he left my mother and married a close family friend soon after. But he had his last drink when I was three, my sister was a baby, and my brothers weren't even born. He worked the program, to use the twelve-step parlance. He carried us further down that path, and my gratitude is immense. If I've been at all helpful to my own kid—and I know I have—it's on the shoulders of my dad's growth, incomplete though it may have been. My work is incomplete, but it builds on his. And if my own children have children, they will benefit from all that growth. I find hope in that.

It's a small example, just one unassuming family tree. But it scales to every family, every community, every civilization. It scales to the movement toward equity and justice.

In Ta-Nehisi Coates's novel *The Water Dancer*, protagonist and former enslaved person Hiram Walker joins an effort to free other enslaved people (whom Coates calls the Tasked). "It occurred to me," Hiram says at one point, "that an examination of the Task revealed not just those evils particular to Virginia, to my old world, but the great need for a new one entirely. Slavery was the root of all struggle . . . this secret war was waged against something more than the Taskmasters of Virginia, that we sought not merely to improve the world, but to remake it."[1] Hiram and his friends do this remaking not by bringing down an entire sick system at once but by freeing one enslaved person at a time.

It's a paradox—each small task we do, whether it's familial or societal, does not remake the world. It makes the present moment better, which is no small thing. But hope infuses those modest acts with meaning, not just to alleviate present suffering, but with the audacious goal to construct a new world.

Some five thousand years ago, a group of people in present-day Ireland took on a monumental project: a tomb one acre across, built with painstaking precision, especially given the technology available at the time. On precisely one day each year—the day of the winter solstice—the sunlight shines through a narrow opening at just the right angle to illumine a sixty-foot corridor where ancient bones and ashes were laid to rest. It's a feat of engineering for a pre-modern people, an act of beauty and devotion. Even today, pilgrims visit Newgrange on the solstice, and even though it's rare for the weather to be sunny enough to activate that perfectly aligned shaft of light, people feel the power of the place.

According to its official website, Newgrange.com, the Stone Age farmers who built Newgrange sought to mark the beginning of the new year. "In addition, it may have served as a powerful symbol of the victory of life over death."

Perhaps. I hope to see it myself someday. But the most powerful symbolism for me lies in how long it took. Archaeologists believe the project took decades, and given that life expectancy was short, this was a task passed down from generation to generation. They imagined something no one had ever seen before, that barely seemed possible. And together, over time, they did it.

Reflect

Explore the idea of hope being generation-level work. Where have you seen this in action?

Practice

Practice taking the long view. Buy a multi-year calendar and look at it regularly. Make a bucket list with more items than you could ever complete. Practice radical patience.

3

Hope Lives in the Body

In the Christian tradition, the resurrection takes central place and top billing—Easter is the highest of the high holy days. But for Christians, the resurrection is meaningless without the incarnation—the belief that God became a human being and dwelled among us, that Jesus was Love in the flesh.

What is doctrine for Christians is nonetheless true of us all: Hope is embodied, or it is nothing at all.

Do we believe that our bodies—their strengths and their frailties—are vessels for hope? And if we do, what does that mean for how we live in them and care for them?

⌁

SELF-CARE IS ALL THE RAGE these days, and for good reason. So many of us are stressed out, despairing over the state of the world and the planet-sized problems we face. Others are just trying to make it through the day. Increased awareness of depression and anxiety means we're more cognizant of the need to pause and take care of ourselves. Our bodies are not machines. We need rest, renewal, relationships.

Self-care is a major topic in our household as we parent kids through the harrowing terrain of adolescence, especially during our daughter's depression. It took time and intention (and many frustrating missteps) to find a healthy mix of self-care, therapeutic work, and the right supports in place, including medication. Today Caroline laughs, plays music, hangs out with friends and family, gets schoolwork done, corrects my improper use of memes, gets mad about injustice, *lives*. We are thankful, even as we take nothing for granted in this life.

As important as it is to be gentle with ourselves, we realized in hindsight how easy it is to lean into those things that are easy but don't provide care so much as comfort. (I'm thankful to writer Sarah Bessey for the language of self-care and self-comfort.)[1] Pajama days, Netflix, a pint of Chunky Monkey for dinner . . . we often label these things as self-care, but they're really self-comfort. They provide relief in the moment. And sometimes that's exactly what we need—and if we're in the throes of despair, it may be all we can manage. We degrade our mental health when we internalize shame over what we "should" be doing. As Mary

Oliver says, "let the soft animal of your body love what it loves."[2] Self-comfort is vital.

Self-*care*, by contrast, is not always fuzzy and comfortable. It may not provide relief in the moment. Self-care can include finding a therapist and going to appointments regularly, taking medication, exercising, grocery shopping so we have nourishing food in the house, or tackling that project that will feel *so good* to get done. (We came to call that "slaying the dragon.")

In the early days of Caroline's depression, we often defaulted to encouraging easy and cozy activities—playing the guitar, taking a nap—rather than working on the looming English assignment or emailing a teacher with a question about an upcoming test. Of course, those things are much, much harder to muster the energy for, and sometimes it just wouldn't have been possible. But the level of relief self-care provides is more lasting than self-comfort. Because once the lavender-scented bath is done, the English assignment is still there.

In other words, there's *feeling* better, and there's *getting* better. You can't do the latter without plenty of the former, but the former often isn't enough in itself.

Then there's the other side, in which we spend so much time doing the things that are helpful for us—the self-care—that we neglect self-comfort. I basically live in this zip code. My mental health and personal productivity benefit from good systems and an uncluttered life and workspace. Calm and order are important to me. So for me, self-care means keeping a decent to-do list (even if I stray from it), tidying the house (sometimes just one room), keeping the fridge stocked, and so on. My days never *stay* neat and tidy, and sometimes the disarray happens within seconds. But constant order isn't the goal—the goal is to start, however briefly, from a calm, centered place, which makes a difference for me.

The thing is, that's a heck of a lot of striving, even in the name of what's good for me. Hope connects to action, but reflexive striving easily overwhelms hope. It becomes all about what *I* can accomplish, what *I* can make happen. When I've neglected self-comfort and gotten out of balance, my body and spirit find ways of letting me know. Robert helps flag this for me: the louder I'm clattering around the kitchen while cooking or doing dishes, the more likely it is that I'm banging against my own weariness and resentment. When that happens, I need self-comfort.

There's plenty to feel hopeless about, and everything feels like an emergency. But hope lives in the body—a finite, human body, or what Paul called treasure in clay jars. Those bodies deserve care and comfort, however we can manage it.

Reflect

What are some of your go-to self-comfort practices? What about self-care?

Practice

Which of the above lists is shorter? Lean into that one for a season and see what happens.

~~~~~~

SITTING ON THE CORNER of my desk is a pair of wireless Bluetooth headphones. For a couple of years they went everywhere with me; I loved the convenience of being able to listen to music, audiobooks, or podcasts while cooking or folding clothes. Now, the battery has degraded enough to render them useless, even with a supposedly full charge. I should get rid of them, but I keep them out of inertia and as an annoyed protest: something so expensive should not be unusable within a couple of years. So there they sit on my desk, a cute ergonomic paperweight with silicon innards.

My sympathetic but gadget-loving husband tells me there's a new version I could buy with better battery life, though they're more expensive, which I'm confident is the point. So-called planned obsolescence is the name of the game in tech. Companies go to market with inexpensive goods which lure buyers into purchasing, but then customers end up spending more down the road because the items must be replaced. Electric toothbrushes are a profligate example in our household. Many fancy homes have an "appliance garage," a place to park the food processors and slow cookers when not being used. What we need is an appliance graveyard. What becomes of a people who prize the shiny and new, bent on replacement when things stop working or simply lose their sheen? What does it say about what we value in ourselves, our relationships, our place on the earth? How does a society built on disposability cultivate a hope that lasts, that doesn't need constant costly upgrades?

Thankfully there's a countermovement, fueled by frugality and environmental concerns, pushing back on a culture buried under new and replacement "stuff." For example, many emergent voices are decrying the effects of "fast fashion," clothing that is cheap and readily available, that prioritizes price and convenience over sustainability, good crafting, fair wages, and a mature supply chain.

With these critics of fast fashion whispering in my ear, I recently cleaned out my closet, intent on keeping only a few versatile, high-quality items. While rummaging through a cedar chest, I ran across a gray wool cardigan I bought while in seminary, a beloved piece of a travel wardrobe I took with me on a January study trip to Geneva. My heart sank when I saw the clusters of moth holes, a casualty of having been forgotten in a dark closet for too many years following that trip. I must have discovered the holes a while back and thrown the sweater in the cedar chest in a moment of "deal with it later."

Thankfully the DIY corners of the Internet have many suggestions for dealing with repairs. There's darning, which I learned in a middle-school home economics class, but I don't feel confident about much of anything I learned in middle school. I could pay professionals to repair it, but with about a dozen holes in a twenty-year-old sweater, it would be a hefty price tag.

I decided to go with felting, which seemed within my abilities as a novice seamstress. Felting involves placing a small ball of rough unspun wool over a hole, putting a foam block underneath it, and using a sharp needle to poke-poke-poke the area so the new fibers integrate with the old frayed ones.

There's a small but growing movement afoot called "right of repair," which encourages companies to develop products in a way that allows them to be repaired by the end user rather than simply replaced (or fixed by a costly specialist). As a grateful patron of the Apple Genius Bar, I'm queasy at the thought of taking a screwdriver to my laptop. But I'm drawn to the idea of repairs being an empowering and inherent right.

Not everything can be repaired, and not everything should be kept. Our possessions can weigh us down. We are experiencing a generational shift as baby boomers retire and downsize, only to discover their children want nothing to do with the delicate china or lumpy sleeper sofas.

But there's something beautiful about refusing to give up on something, whether it's an old sweater, a relationship, or a nation. I'm jarred by the old phrase "America: love it or leave it." Do we not also have the right of repair of our country? While eccentric billionaires plot their escape to space when the earth isn't inhabitable anymore, the climate crisis turns on a fundamental right of repair of the planet—for everyone. This is what we're fighting for. This is what we're hoping for.

Besides, a right-to-repair society feels like a kinder place to live, where flaws are celebrated as markers of uniqueness, ingenuity, and resilience. My sweater fixes are visible, but I've decided to welcome the flaws as part of what makes this garment unique. My sweater has a history and I embrace it. (Next step: embracing my own middle-aged body and its history, evident in every curve and wrinkle.)

Right of repair extends to our lives and our very bodies. COVID-19 has exposed our physical vulnerability in many unsettling (but perhaps important) ways. At the same time, I'm constantly astounded at how strong our bodies really are. When someone has cancer, we inject them with poison. How could anyone come back from such an assault? And yet people do, every day. The matriarch of our family broke her leg at age ninety-eight. Not only were surgeons able to repair it, but she was up and walking (carefully, with support) within days. Results may vary—and do. Positive health outcomes are not evenly distributed across all races or ethnicities. All the more reason to embrace right of repair for everyone. We have a right to flourish and persist. Nobody should be cast aside.

We all have our share of ragged and frayed spots, brought about by neglect, lack of self-care, or even trauma. We may shove the evidence of those injuries in a drawer for a long time because we just can't deal with them. When we're finally ready to repair, we need to let go of expectations of returning to a pristine or untouched "before." The felted places on my sweater are a little bulky and scratchy to the touch, a reminder of my imperfect handiwork. But just as a bone fracture can heal stronger than before, I suspect the felted places will be the most resilient.

Elisabeth Kubler-Ross wrote, "The most beautiful people we have known are those who have known defeat, known suffering, known struggle, known loss, and have found their way out of the depths. These persons have an appreciation, a sensitivity, and an understanding of life that fills them with compassion, gentleness, and a deep loving concern. Beautiful people do not just happen."[1]

But when they do—that's hope's loving and messy handiwork.

Reflect

How is your physical space (your home/office/car) a reflection of you and what you value? How does it reflect a hopeful outlook?

Practice

Go on a walk in nature or near your home. Find an "imperfect" object—a leaf with a tear in it, a misshapen rock—and put it in a prominent place as a reminder that even irregular things can be useful and beautiful.

The Power of Anger

I GOT MY FIRST TATTOO at the ripe old age of forty-eight. It took a while to decide on a design, but I settled on a quote from my favorite book from childhood, *A Wrinkle in Time*. When Meg Murry prepares to battle the evil monster IT and rescue her brother from its clutches, a wise older mentor tells her: "You have something that IT has not."[1] That something ends up saving the day.

This line is now on my arm. But there's another quote I like almost as much, also uttered by one of the mentor crones:

"Stay angry, little Meg. You will need all your anger now."[2]

I can't bring myself to tattoo it on my body.

Yet.

I've been pretty mad on and off for the past several years. In my defense, there's plenty of large and small injustices to be angry about. Social media makes the whole world our neighborhood; every racist outburst at Trader Joe's or unruly mob at a school board meeting is there for us to see, and every desperate refugee denied asylum and shelter might as well be on our own doorstep. During the pandemic, a teacher friend asked if she could prop her door open to increase ventilation and was instructed not to because closed doors are safer in case of an active shooter. How is this the world? Meanwhile, "How dare you?" thunders a teenage girl to the United Nations in a speech about the climate crisis. How, indeed.

I love the idea that Meg Murry's anger isn't a liability but a gift, but I also feel sheepish trumpeting the power of anger. Yes, Jesus overturns the tables in the temple in a fit of righteous indignation, but God's nature is repeatedly described as *slow* to anger. "Be angry, but do not sin" suggests that anger is natural, but we're told elsewhere to put anger away (Col. 3:8). Spiritually, anger is complicated stuff. Anger becomes a source of shame—shame inflected by gender (women aren't supposed to be angry), race and class (what do *I* as a privileged White person have to be angry about), relationality (geez, why don't you lighten up, it's not that bad), and personality (I'm a One on the Enneagram, and we suppress anger at all costs). And the real secret: anger is often grief in disguise, and this grief is crushing: we are so far from the world as it should be.

But anger can also be a powerful fuel, not just for action but for hope itself.

Valarie Kaur is a Sikh activist, filmmaker, and lawyer, whose work began in earnest following the murder of a Sikh family friend, the first person killed in a hate crime after 9/11. She tells her story and explores faithful activism in her book *See No Stranger: A Memoir and Manifesto of Revolutionary Love.*

As much as I'm drawn to Kaur's work, I found myself bristling at the word *love* in the title. I've been burned by too many treatises on a love that makes no place for righteous anger, that divorces itself from the quest for justice.

A quick flip through the table of contents won me over. Kaur devotes an entire chapter, in a book about revolutionary love, to the topic of rage. Not just anger—rage. In it she cites the work of neurobiologists who study oxytocin, or the love hormone. A high level of oxytocin correlates to nurturing behavior in mammals, especially toward their young. It also decreases aggression—"With one exception," Kaur writes: "in defense of her young. When babies are threatened, oxytocin actually increases aggression. For mothers, rage is part of love: it is the biological force that protects that which is loved."[3]

Yes, rage can devour us from the inside, but it can also give us the courage and strength to act. Rage is a healthy and necessary response to threat. It is a rightful, bodily reaction.

My favorite character in the Harry Potter books is Tonks, a gutsy, fierce hunter of so-called dark wizards—those allied with the villainous supremacist Voldemort. (She's also able to magically alter her physical features. How can you not love a character who can make her hair bright pink or give her nose a piggish shape?) On a recent reread of the final book, I caught a detail I had missed about the timing of the final show-down with Voldemort, called the battle of Hogwarts. Tonks gives birth to a son, Teddy Lupin, sometime in the spring, and the battle occurs near the end of the school year. (The dates aren't specified in the books, though fans have posited April for the birth, May for the battle.)

Tonks—postpartum Tonks, her body still healing, still leaking breast milk and perhaps even blood—is a part of that battle. Nobody would have begrudged her for sitting this one out. But she couldn't. This was the fight of their lives, and it ended up costing her life.

The close timing of birth and battle affected me deeply, perhaps more deeply than a fiction book should. It points to a real-life truth: that we don't always get to choose the hows and whens of our service and sacrifice. We don't always have the luxury of being rested and ready. And as someone who's given birth three times myself, I wonder: had Tonks been recovered and healed after such an arduous physical ordeal, maybe she wouldn't have perished in the fighting. But Kaur's reminder about the power that resides in our own bodies leads me to a more empowering conclusion: Tonks's body contained abundant strength because she was fighting for the people she loved most. What Teddy needed was a world free of Voldemort's evil, and that's what Tonks lived and died for. We are fierce and we are finite, a paradox that leaves me both heartbroken and hopeful.

I'm still not sure about getting an anger tattoo on my body. "You have something that IT has not" already requires enough explanation for interested strangers. But that "something," I'm always happy to tell people, is love. And anger is a component of love, and one to be trusted and even nurtured.

Reflect

How were you taught to express anger as a child—or were you? What's your connection to anger now? Do you see anger as fuel, or something to be avoided?

Practice

On slips of paper, write down some of the things that make you angry. Let them go in a ritual of release: burn them, immerse them in water, rip them up. See what you experience when you do.

I HEARD THE LOUD THUNK but didn't pay it much mind until my son came to find me. A chickadee had hit the sliding door leading to our deck.

By the time I got there, it had righted itself and was standing, feathers ruffled, head cocked upward, beak open as if gulping the air. My heart softened at the bird, and at my son's immediate desire to help. Sensing that his intervention might have frightened it further, he knelt down, the offending glass separating them, and sat vigil.

I wondered at the evolutionary impulses at work. The bird was vulnerable, too dazed to fly away. Did the angle of the bird's neck make respiration easier, like when tilting a person's chin upward to open the airway during rescue breathing? Did the puffed-up feathers give it the appearance of being bigger and thus warn off predators? Did the upward gaze allow it some small vigilance if danger approached, enough time for one desperate attempt at escape? Perhaps the poor thing was simply in shock, which birds experience just as humans and other animals do. I remembered my first aid training for shock: Keep the person still. Loosen clothing. Cover with a blanket.

As a teenager, I stubbed my bare foot into a wall at high speed, breaking my little toe. Within minutes I felt nauseous and chilled. Like that bird, standing stock still, I dared not move as the world spun around me. But the physical shock coincided with an emotional shock. I'd been running to the phone to call to try and win concert tickets. Something so silly, and then out of nowhere: pain. Then came a second wave of mental shock as I saw my toe sticking out at a sickening angle from my foot. *I don't understand. I was supposed to be the fifteenth caller.*

That was my most vivid experience of physiological shock. (I've been lucky.) But there have been more profound emotional shocks. My parents' divorce remains the greatest. I don't know whether my parents seemed genuinely happy to me, whether I coasted on a distorted view of statistics (yes, almost half of all marriages end in divorce, but it hadn't happened to anyone I knew, so it must be a phenomenon for "other people"), or whether I didn't allow myself to consider that my entire life could change so fully. Whatever the reason, a separation, divorce, and move from my childhood home while in middle school—the *middle* of middle school, to be clear—would have been unthinkable. When the impossible became possible, it was like flying headlong into a clear glass window, mistaking it for more trees, more open air to naively traverse.

When the room is spinning and the mind is reeling with "this isn't right, I'm hurt," often the next step is stillness and silence. It's not a tactical defeat; it's a necessary move toward hope and healing.

Friends had been telling me for months to check out the Nap Ministry. "You've written about Sabbath-keeping and self-care, you'll really appreciate it," they said. I nodded and blew them off, thinking it was yet another attempt to commodify Sabbath by equating it with pedicures and organic cotton sheets with high thread counts.

I couldn't have been more wrong—nor more excited to be wrong. The Nap Ministry is the brainchild of "nap bishop" Tricia Hersey, a Black artist and activist who curates "nap installations" and other programs around the country as an antidote and protest against constant work, consumption, and a "grind" mentality, which Hersey argues is a tool of White-supremacy culture. "Disrupt and push back against a system that views you as a machine," Hersey writes. "You are not a machine. You are a divine human being. WE WILL REST."[1]

Constant activity does violence to the body and soul. Sometimes we're stopped by our bodies saying "no more." Other times we run smack into hard glass, smack into ourselves. Hersey credits her grandmother for inspiring the Nap Ministry; no matter how busy and burdened she was, she took time each day to close her eyes to restore, to let the blunt-force traumas of the day subside.

With each passing minute our chickadee stood there drinking the air, the more worried I got. *Why can't it fly away?* But I also marveled at its ability simply to stand. In fact, maybe its willingness to rest for as long as needed boded well for it.

How much time is enough? Our bodies usually know.

I later read, too late to be useful, that when birds are in shock from a window collision, you can carefully cradle them and put them in a box and let them recover in quiet darkness until they are ready to take flight again. Many birds will be able to fly away after that period of rest. But even then, there may be underlying conditions, concussions and the like, that make prognosis poor. Millions of birds each year simply don't make it.

By the time we left for an outing about thirty minutes later, the bird was standing quietly in place, still not moving, but breathing normally and seemingly still at rest. When we returned a couple of hours later, it was gone. I hope it benefited from being on a deck, sheltered from view of owls or other predators, and simply flew away when it was ready. But who really knows? And who knows whether it survived the next few days or succumbed to injuries we couldn't see?

Emily Dickinson compared hope to "the thing with feathers / that perches in the soul, / and sings the tune without the words / and never stops—at all."[2] Sometimes. Sometimes the singing stops. Studies suggest that chickadees that have encountered a predator will retain a memory of that predator, and it even impacts their success at bearing offspring.

There's a kind of hope that is carefree. I would argue that it's a less mature version of hope. Sometimes the world shocks us, and we aren't always better for it. We never fly with as much abandon as we do before colliding with the window. But with time and stillness, we may gain the strength to take flight again.

Reflect

Reflect kindly and gently on your own experiences of physical or emotional shock. Where do these experiences still live in your body?

Practice

Make some time each day for stillness and quiet. If ten minutes is too much, start with five. Or one.

PART OF MY WORK as a leadership coach over the past few years has been to consult with a variety of groups doing antiracism work. Most are religious-based organizations seeking to root out and dismantle the systems of oppression that have been in place for a long time but that many folks have only recently begun to see clearly.

I remember a meeting with a group that was relatively new at this. (Truth be told, so am I.) You could tell people were feeling the weight of the task, the urgency of the work, and the vulnerability it would require. They were bound to stumble and misstep, something none of us enjoys. All kinds of things would need to be picked over and examined. It's also generation-level work; we will not dismantle all oppressive systems in our lifetime. I could see people's shoulders dropping by the minute. It's just so much.

Finally one person sighed and said, "Does this get any easier?"

At the time, I affirmed the feeling and urged both courage and compassion. Later though, I remembered a bit of wisdom I once heard from an elite-level runner:

It doesn't get easier.
You just get stronger.

When you're first starting out as a runner, going a mile without stopping is an incredible feat. Over time though, you build up more endurance, and that endurance moves you to try new things: *I've run two miles. Could I run three? I run four times a week. Could I stretch it to five? Could I do that mile thirty seconds faster? Could I run safely into my sixties? Seventies? Beyond?* (Consider the example of "Miss Ida" Keeling, an eighty-three-pound great-grandmother and the author of *Can't Nothing Bring Me Down*, who ran until she was north of 105 years old.)

But no matter how long you've been at it, there's going to be some discomfort. You never outgrow it. If you're doing your best, performing as well as you're able, it takes effort, whether you're Meb Keflezighi or yours truly. (Go stand on the sidelines of mile twenty-two of a marathon if you don't believe me. Any smiles you see are actually grimaces.) Even if you're just going out to run some joy miles, it's still tough going. Couches are *comfortable*.

So it is with antiracism work, or any work worth doing, any effort that imagines a better world. So long as we're on this journey, there will always be at least some discomfort, whether it's a hitch in the throat or a churn in the stomach. But our capacity will also be growing, and there's a lot of hope in that. So it'll be new stuff, more impactful stuff, that triggers the discomfort. And the process brings its own wisdom and a deep satisfaction that tempers some of the discomfort.

Just recently, a White friend with whom I share this work got lovingly challenged by a Black colleague for something she said. It didn't feel good—stumbles never do—but she's been at this awhile, so she was able to receive the feedback and learn from it. She also knew enough to take some time to let the experience sink in and give herself some grace and care.

We're living through a time of tremendous change. The past few years have had an indelible effect on us all. (I suspect that will be true no matter when you pick up this book.) The next era has yet to be written because we're in the process of writing it.

The bad news is, it doesn't get easier.

The good news is, we do get stronger.

Just so we're clear: I kinda hate this. I like to commiserate with that same friend about "FGOs." (The second two letters are "growth opportunity"; the first letter is easily guessed.) FGOs aren't fun. But hopeful people know, safety isn't a part of the deal. Discomfort isn't a sign to stop. It's a sign to lean in further.

And part of getting stronger, in running or in life, is learning when you're pushing *too* hard, knowing when it's time to take a break. It's actually during the recovery time that muscles get stronger and capacity increases.

So do the work, itchy though it may be, and claim time for rest.

See the world as it is and savor the joy in striving to make it better.

Reflect

Reflect on the running mantra, "It doesn't get easier, you just get stronger." What do you know how to do now that you didn't know ten years ago? Five years? One year? Six months? Yesterday?

Practice

Find a friend and commit to an FGO together. (It's more fun with a buddy!)

Trauma = Pain + Confusion

~~~~~~

SEVERAL YEARS AGO, I slammed the rear door of my minivan on my daughter's head. Hard.

We were in the kiss-and-ride line before school and it was orchestra day, which meant a small kid maneuvering a big cello out of the car and into the school. I felt the long line of cars behind me, and the busyness of the day ahead of me, as I hustled to open the back hatch, unload the cello, and get on my way. I expected Caroline to be waiting on the sidewalk or beside the car, but a split second after pulling down on the door with forceful efficiency, I saw the kid at my left elbow. I'll never forget the sound.

We both started crying—a lot.

At the suggestion of a pediatrician friend, I checked Caroline out of school for a day of brain rest. Everything turned out fine, though I still shudder when I think of it.

When I asked about it recently, Caroline's response was to laugh. Apparently, it wasn't too traumatic. But the issue of trauma is a complicated one. Interest in the topic has exploded in recent years, but what is it?

I've heard trauma described in this way:

First, think about the experience of pain. We feel it for as long as it lasts, and then hopefully it ends. We may remember the sensations— I recall *exactly* what labor and childbirth felt like, contrary to claims that people forget—but the pain probably doesn't continue to have undue power over us.

Now think about confusion: the way we feel when the world as we know it changes and our understanding of life has fundamentally shifted. Confusion, like pain, can take a while to get over, and it may or may not continue to reverberate, but it can be worked through.

Trauma, in very simple terms, is the combination of pain plus confusion.

More than the tears on Caroline's face when the door came crashing down, I will never forget the look of shocked betrayal: *How could my mother, the person I trust most in the world, hurt me this way?* The relationship was repaired quickly enough, partly because it was clear how remorseful I was. It was an honest mistake, and I conveyed lots of care and love in the aftermath, which my daughter received. But the confusion had to be resolved somehow, a new understanding of the world reached: *Yes, I can trust my mother more than anyone in the world, and she would never seek to do me harm, but she's also human.*

For many people, watching the halls of the Capitol be overrun by an angry mob in early 2021 and realizing that many of them intended great harm, even, perhaps, a coup, caused many of us profound emotional pain. Some of that emotional pain even manifested physically. But coupled with that pain was an intense confusion: *How could this happen? How is this America? How did we get to this point? What do we do now?*

It's going to take a lot of time to sort it out. I hope we can. Recent years have revealed how little capacity many of us have for pain and confusion. We love to numb the former and gloss over the latter with easy answers or denial. To paraphrase Daniel Pink, we'll choose false certainty over genuine ambiguity any time.[1]

When pain and confusion run rampant, it's hard to have hope. But even people carrying trauma can begin to feel hope again. For Resmaa Menakem, therapist and author of *My Grandmother's Hands: Racialized Trauma and the Pathway to Mending Our Hearts and Bodies,* trauma is at the root of our country's racism—not just trauma for Black bodies but

trauma among White people and also law enforcement. His book is a
handbook on healing this trauma, and it starts with the body.[2]

Many years ago, while in college, my youngest brother worked for a
Subway sandwich shop. One night during his shift, the store was robbed
at gunpoint. It all turned out OK—Luke cooperated with the man, handing over the small amount of money in the register, then calling the police long after the man departed. As I remember it, Luke described going
into a kind of autopilot. It was only later that he let himself absorb how
much danger he'd faced.

After the incident, I mentioned it to a friend and spiritual mentor of
mine because I was feeling rattled myself. My friend is a therapist, and
she offered advice, which I dutifully relayed to him: "Tell him to get out
for some vigorous exercise as soon as he possibly can. Ideally something
that gets the heartrate up, the blood pumping, and the muscles burning.
He's been through a trauma and his body has been flooded with adrena-
line. He needs to clear that out and replace it with some endorphins."

While I don't know much about the adrenaline-to-endorphins
thing, I do know firsthand the power of catharsis that can only come
through the body. I'm a big believer in therapy and mindfulness and
self-comfort and all the rest, but we carry around so much of this stuff
subcutaneously.

Ruby Sales is a veteran civil-rights activist who focuses on community building as a spiritual enterprise. She remembers a turning point in
her journey while at the beauty salon. The hairdresser's daughter came
in that morning, weighed down from a long night hustling on the streets.
Moved to compassion, Sales asked her, "Where does it hurt?" With that
simple question, years of pain poured out. We carry so much pain, and
we carry it in our bodies.[3]

We can find our way to hope, but there's no mental shortcut. Healing
can happen, but it relies on our being willing to acknowledge the pain
and live in the genuine ambiguity for a while.

We rest. We weep. We dance and run and box and bike. And we find
glimmers of promise.

Reflect

Explore the idea of trauma as connected to pain and confusion. How do you see this definition at work in our broader culture?

Practice

Whatever your experience with trauma, find some body-oriented practices that feel good to you (walking, tai chi, dancing, etc.).

Low-Power Mode

~~~~~~

WE'RE IN THIS WORK of hope-building for the duration, which means we need to pace ourselves for the long haul. One way to start is to borrow a strategy from our devices and activate low-power mode. I discovered this technological feature when my phone's battery started malfunctioning such that I barely made it more than half a day without running down to zero.

Low-power mode allows our cell phones to be operational for a lot longer between battery charges by ratcheting back a few key features:

The phone runs a bit slower.
Screen brightness is reduced and some visual effects are disabled.
The phone auto-locks or powers down more quickly when idle.

For many of us, the COVID-19 pandemic was an experience of low-power mode. We moved more slowly. It didn't take much to overload us. The world, perhaps, felt a little dimmer: no large boisterous gatherings, less chit-chat in the grocery store, fewer hugs. I found myself powering down much more quickly: going to bed early, napping, indulging in lighthearted TV shows and beloved books I'd already read because the thought of something new was too much. (One man I know revisited the 1980s sitcom *Golden Girls*: "I already know these people," he rationalized.) And yes, I locked up from time to time, sniping irritably at the people around me.

You can tell your phone is set to low-power mode because the battery icon is yellow. The symbolism couldn't be clearer: *caution.*

Here's my favorite part: in low-power mode, apps don't run in the background anymore. Auto-fetching of email doesn't happen, for example. Remarkable! We create these machines to be efficient and seamless multitaskers, but even they have their limits. As for humans, multitasking has always been an illusion, a fiction we tell ourselves—at best, we switch quickly between tasks, usually at the expense of accuracy and equanimity—but quarantine really laid this fiction bare. I couldn't keep as many balls in the air as I usually do (and believe me, I tried). That diminished capacity persists even today.

I fret sometimes when I think about the problems we must face as a society—as a planet—right now, when nobody seems to be at their best. The work is immense and it won't wait for us to charge up to 100 percent. But therein lies an opportunity: maybe low-power mode isn't an impediment to a changed world, but the very gift we need to transform a culture of striving and grinding and endless production into something more humane.

Activist Valarie Kaur likes to say, "The way we make change is just as important as the change we make."[1] My coaching clients may be tired of hearing me repeat that, but so long as people rationalize their short-cutting of relationships and empathy (especially empathy for self) in the name of getting "important" things done, I'll keep using it. When I'm treading hard rather than living lightly, it remains my mantra too. In low-power mode, we dare to imagine a world that can be better, even if it means downshifting our heroic efforts a bit.

Some of us find it all too easy to judge ourselves for having reduced battery life. Hopeful people should always be "on," especially when there's so much to do. But if diminished capacity can happen to technology, it is certainly acceptable for flesh-and-blood creatures. Environmental activists teach that we need millions of people doing sustainability imperfectly, not a few people doing it perfectly. We have the tools we need to survive this: rest, reflection, simplicity, community, grace. Low-power mode is enough. Shockingly, we may find we are well made for this moment.

Reflect

How do you know when your body is entering low-power mode? What are your most obvious signs?

Practice

On a sheet of paper, draw an energy gauge like a gas tank. Pay attention to where you are at various points throughout the day. Notice what draws down your energy and what replenishes it. Are there ways to minimize the former or maximize the latter? (Sometimes the answer is no.) What else do you notice?

WHEN DID I KNOW our kid's depression had retreated? There were many signposts along the way. One of my favorites happened when Caroline received a history assignment to watch a piece of pop culture that reflected the historical period they had studied and analyze it for accuracies, inaccuracies, and social commentary.

Despite the open-endedness, this was not a welcome assignment. It was late in the year and a mighty senioritis had set in. Nonetheless Caroline gamely made a choice: *Monty Python and the Holy Grail.*

My daughter has always had a single dimple on one cheek, which led Robert and me to coin a phrase: when Caroline laughs really hard, that's called "deep dimple fun."

Monty Python was deep dimple fun for our eighteen-year-old kid, following a time when we hadn't seen the dimple much. The film was silly and dumb and chockablock with actors committing their whole hearts to the single task of making people laugh. (And it had enough historical content, however skewed, to write a decent paper to graduate.)

Laughter, joy, play—these are essential for cultivating hope. They are also acts of resistance. "I am the darker brother," writes Langston Hughes in his poem "I, Too." He knows he is seen as a second-class citizen, without a seat at the table. "But I laugh, / And eat well, / And grow strong."[1]

Laughter and joy are often the first things to go when everything hits the fan. After the recent pandemic, a pastor friend commented that his congregation desperately needed to play together but seemed too wrung out to do so. He worried they had forgotten how.

Play helps establish the pathway thinking we talked about in an earlier section of this book. The people I know who play most readily (and laugh most easily) are some of the most hopeful people I know. The late Molly Ivins spent her career writing about the often-ludicrous machinations of the Texas legislature, which she dubbed the "lege." She died some years ago of breast cancer, but many Molly-isms live on in the hearts of her fans, including this gem: "Keep fighting for freedom and justice, beloveds, but don't forget to have fun doin' it. Rejoice in all the oddities that freedom can produce. And when you get through celebrating the sheer joy of a good fight, be sure to tell those who come after how much fun it was!"[2]

Laughter is physiological as well as spiritual. When we laugh, a variety of muscles contract and relax, which can ease tension and even chronic pain. Studies suggest laughter can boost the immune system. "You know what I like about comedy?" asks Stephen Colbert. "You can't laugh and be afraid at the same time . . . of anything. If you're laughing, I defy you to be afraid."[3]

The Harry Potter series explores this link between fear and laughter through a fascinating creature called a boggart. A boggart is a shape-shifter—it takes the form of whatever the person fears most, which means that the boggart looks different to every person.

The incantation against a boggart is the word "Riddikulus!" But the incantation alone isn't enough; one must also imagine something funny, something that makes the person laugh. The boggart then morphs from something scary into something, well, ridiculous. Giant spiders suddenly skitter about on roller skates. A cobra turns into a jack-in-the-box.

Laughter can wound. Laughter can also heal. But it's not easy to find the joy when we're under stress.

What could possibly make someone laugh in the midst of the fear? How can we stare into the face of what terrifies us and see it as something absurd rather than frightening?

We can do this if we know that, while the fear is very real to us, it is not ultimately true. What is true? For me, it is what Paul wrote to the early church in Rome: that there is nothing, not death, nor evil, nor things present, nor things to come, nor powers, nor hopelessness, that will be able to separate us from the love of God in Christ.

Seminary professor Tom Long tells a story about the city of Atlanta during the civil rights movement—how the Ku Klux Klan would often march down Auburn Avenue, which was the African-American center of town. Each time the people would see the Klan coming they would draw their shades, lock their doors, and cower in their homes in the dark, silent and still, until that parade of evil was over.

And it was like that for a long, long time.

Meanwhile, those people on Auburn Avenue and in Montgomery and Birmingham and Selma and so many other places held tightly to a promise that despair and destruction would not be the end of the story.

And then, slowly and quickly and slowly and quickly, civil rights started to take hold.

When people could finally see justice on the horizon, the Klan marched once again down Auburn Avenue. But this time the people lifted their window shades, threw open their doors, stood on the sidewalk and laughed, and laughed, and laughed. And the Klan never marched down Auburn Avenue again.[4]

Ridikkulus.

Reflect

"Laughter is physiological as well as spiritual." When was the last time you laughed or experienced deep joy? Describe it as fully as you can, savoring it as you do.

Practice

Set ten minutes on the clock and make a list of things that bring you joy—name as many as you can. Then take a different-colored pen and circle the things you haven't experienced recently. Pick one and make a plan to pursue it.

4

Hope Travels in Story

A teenager was preparing to go through the confirmation process, the Christian rite of passage in which young people claim their faith as their own, independent of their parents. She went to her father, who happened to be the pastor, and said she wasn't sure she believed everything she was supposed to believe. She still had lots of questions and doubts.

Her father said, "What you promise when you are confirmed is not that you will believe this forever. What you promise when you are confirmed is that this is the story you will wrestle with forever."[1]

Whether Christian or not, our lives are made up of stories. These narratives give our lives meaning, shape, and purpose.

This section considers hope not as an emotion or an action but as a rich story. What kind of story are you writing with your life? Is it a hopeful one? How?

~~~~~~

WHEN OUR KIDS WERE LITTLE, we cycled through a series of bedtime songs that included "Puff the Magic Dragon," the Peter, Paul, and Mary song about a boy and a dragon and their good times aboard the dragon's ship. The song ends on a melancholy note, with Jackie outgrowing his adventures with Puff. Sometimes my kids would express sadness at this ending, often asking us to sing it again from the top. Were they confronting the existential realities of life, death, and loss in an age-appropriate manner? Or did they want to delay lights out as long as possible? Probably both.

One night, on a whim, I improvised an addendum to the song:

> But then Puff met three children, you all know their names,
> Caroline and Margaret too, and then comes little James,
> They climbed aboard that dragon ship
>   and Puff became their friend.
> And so the song goes on and on, it never has to end.

As a parent of little kids, it felt good to keep the narrative going. Now those little ones are teens and the melancholy has caught up to me. The song did end. I haven't sung either version in a long time. But I imagine, sometime in the future, the song could pick up again with grandchildren or other little ones in my life.

Hope is not an outcome, a product, or a projection.

Hope, first and foremost, is a story we live in, a story we cultivate and perpetuate. It's a story with characters who help us along the way and, sadly, some who harm us—maybe villainously so. There are challenges and climaxes and cliffhangers and codas. The story, like the revised Puff, goes on and on.

With grim regularity, some climate agency will publish a report reassessing the risks and impacts of climate change. I have yet to see one in which they say, "Oops, it's actually not as bad as we thought before." The estimates are always trending in a grim direction.

People respond to these reports in a variety of ways. Sadly, some still deny the problem and our role in it, but even those of us who believe the science are often tempted to ignore the facts. It's easy to feel fatalism and despair. It's simultaneously the best news—we have the tools to mitigate the effects—and the worst—if we don't do it, no one will.

But we've got to get our minds right about it. The problem with climate is it's such a big comprehensive issue, and the news is so grave, that even good-intentioned people who'd want to do something about it feel frozen in place. Climate scientists are starting to realize this and adjust how they talk about the problem. "I think there's [a] danger that we decide we're doomed, let's despair, let's not even try," says Kate Marvel, a climate scientist at Columbia University and NASA. "I find that almost as frightening as not doing anything because we don't believe it's happening."[1]

So Marvel did an unusual thing: she wrote a fairy tale.

The story she wrote centers around a dragon who rampages across the land. (Not a friendly dragon like Puff the magic one.) The dragon breathes fire and sets the countryside aflame. Its expansive wings stir up torrential winds. The dragon terrorizes the people, making them cower in their homes.

And the king? "The king accepted this and prepared once again to do nothing."

Sounds familiar. But then there's a surprise twist: "The kingdom does not retreat. Heroes challenge the dragon repeatedly. When they fall, others rise to take their place. They know their quest is a doomed one. They set out, nevertheless."

And here is the ending: "They did not all live happily ever after, but they lived. And most importantly, they had something to live for."

Thinking about hope as a narrative—as a story in which we live our lives—helps give us something to live for.

As we continue to be embroiled in conflict over our nation's racial reckoning, it seems that we're really arguing over what story to tell about ourselves. There are competing narratives. One tends to center around our nation as a valiant hero. Sure, there have been missteps—every hero has a shadow side—but good has always prevailed and the hero triumphed.

Then there's the competing narrative of our nation, more complicated, told primarily through voices of those who haven't traditionally narrated it. The hero, it turns out, is deeply flawed. Maybe he isn't a hero at all, but simply a protagonist, still on a journey to find himself and do better. Or maybe the story has different heroes altogether: the scores of oppressed people who, despite obstacles, have persisted and want to see the story turn out differently, to be a happier ending for all.

I find the latter story much more truthful. I've also seen how it instantly turns people off. Yet we must keep telling it, refining it as we go, never compromising on our history but giving people of good will a place to find themselves in it, so we can write a redemptive next chapter.

The psychiatrist Bessel van der Kolk has spent his life studying and teaching about trauma; much of his work is captured in the book *The Body Keeps the Score*. Part of the therapeutic process for victims of trauma is dealing with the past and telling a new story about it. "The way we deal with unpleasant situations is by imagining how we can do things differently," he says. "Trauma destroys that capacity to imagine how things can be different. . . . So a very big issue in helping people to overcome trauma is to experience the possibility of alternative outcomes."[2]

Stories can be powerful motivators, whether we've experienced trauma or not. When we consider the competing stories of our nation, the conflict often gets reduced to one side being too optimistic, the other too pessimistic. We get beyond this unhelpful impasse by framing a truthful story in a way that yields hope. Which stories empower us to live better and embody our nation's ideals, in deed as well as in word? What stories help us make meaning of our lives, recognizing that lots of diverse people make up that "our"? Right now, the challenge seems insurmountable, the gulf between people quite vast. And there are powerful interests who benefit from our division into Us and Them. But the work of hopeful narration is the work of our time.

Reflect

Reflect on the idea of hope being an element of story. What does this idea open up for you? What do you still wonder about?

Practice

Choose a pivotal or challenging time of your life and write it as a story. Give it a beginning, middle, and end, with challenges and obstacles, and you as the protagonist. How does this exercise give you a different insight into what happened and how you prevailed or simply survived? (Bonus: Plan a communal gathering for sharing these stories.)

Telling the Right Kind of Story

~~~~~~

STORIES GIVE OUR LIVES MEANING and shape, but some convey hope more effectively than others. Science-fiction author Ted Chiang has explored the difference between what he calls conservative and progressive stories. (In this context, conservative and progressive aren't partisan/political distinctions but reflect how stories are constructed and how they resolve.)

Conservative stories follow this format:

The world starts out as a good place.
Evil intrudes.
Good defeats evil.
The world goes back to being a good place.

Progressive stories, by contrast, follow this pattern:

The world starts out as a familiar place.
A new discovery or invention disrupts everything.
The world is forever changed.[1]

On a superficial level, a lot of Christian dogma appears to follow the conservative structure. We are burdened by sin, and by accepting Christ as our savior, we can be guaranteed a place in heaven, the ultimate "good place." Even Christian churches that de-emphasize personal salvation have conservative stories that creep into everyday practice. I've worked with churches that tell certain stories on a loop: tales of their vibrant past when the pews were full and the Sunday School classes overflowing. Intellectually, they know that story is over, but in their hearts, they yearn to go back to that "good place" of the past, and the conservative framing of the story keeps them stuck.

The Christian story, by contrast, is deeply progressive. It begins in a garden populated by two people and concludes in a city teeming with folks from north and south, east and west. Along the way there are disruptions: enslavement, plague, exodus, conquest, scandal, exile, birth, ministry, death, resurrection, more ministry, persecution, conversion, mission.

And the world is never the same.

Jesus's death and resurrection don't restore creation to a static condition. Those who follow the way of Christ are called to a new way of life in service to others, an expansive ministry of grace. The resurrection, in other words, isn't the solution to a problem but the introduction of a whole new set of problems: how do we live in a world that is forever changed?

Conservative stories are precious and have their place. There's a satisfying sense of closure when the heroes win and the villains lose. But these stories also fundamentally preserve the status quo—once the obstacle is vanquished, we can go back to living our lives as before. Comforting, but not helpful in a world of constant change.

The 1977 film *Superman* starring Christopher Reeve exemplifies a beloved story that follows the conservative pattern. At the climax, the Man of Steel literally reverses the rotation of the earth to turn back time and undo a disaster that has killed millions of people, including his sweetheart, Lois Lane. He defeats the arch-villain Lex Luthor and vanquishes his evil plot, but the end of the film sees us in much the same safe place as when we started—we now have a superhero who can swoop in and set things back to rights through the promotion of "truth, justice, and the American Way."

Progressive stories are more ambiguous and may not provide the same catharsis. They leave the door open for unsatisfying endings. The world is forever changed, which could be positive or negative. (The current popularity of dystopian fiction suggests that the latter is winning out; we seem to be bracing for the worst, gripped by a collectively gloomy mood.)

Progressive stories may be more realistic—they reflect the way the world usually works—but that often makes them, paradoxically, more intriguing. The status quo is blown apart, and what's left in its wake *may* be doom and dystopia, or it could hold the potential for transformation. A lot of this depends on us, and it depends on where we're located. As Chiang says, "Aristocrats might have thought the world was ending when feudalism was abolished during the French Revolution, but the world didn't end; the world changed."[2]

Like *Superman*, 2012's Marvel movie *The Avengers* ends happily, with a nascent team of heroes, gods, and superspies banding together to put down a threat, this time from outer space. But *The Avengers* leans more progressive than its superhero precursor because the world is different, and all is not well. The people of Earth now know they're not alone in the universe—they are vulnerable as never before—and the very heroes that saved the day also make their world a target for future attacks. The strains of triumph are tempered by an unease that something has fundamentally changed.

Subsequent Marvel movies explore these progressive themes in some pretty sophisticated ways, addressing questions of power and accountability. Commentator and podcaster Van Lathan Jr. says, "Captain America could easily be a very dangerous figure. The nation's top policeman, essentially—top soldier—who takes unilateral action, does things based on his set of values, makes decisions that affect millions, billions of people. . . . If the wrong guy has that power, that guy could be a lethal entity to society."[3]

Progressive stories require a different kind of protagonist. Recent years have seen a rise in superheroes who are queer, female, and non-White, including a Black Superman. These characters have existed in comic books for decades but are now appearing onscreen for the mass public. There's a profit motive at work for sure—studios know that diverse casts mean more patrons and a wider audience—but it also means the stories can break open in powerful ways. Representation matters.

Consider the shift in Captain America from Steve Rogers, a White man who assumed the mantle in the 1940s, to Sam Wilson, who is Black, in the present day. "I'm a Black man wearing the stars and stripes," Sam says in one iteration of his story. "Every time I [pick up the shield], I know there are millions of people out there who are gonna hate me for it. . . . And there's nothing I can do to change it. Yet, I'm still here. . . . The only power I have is that I believe we can do better."[4]

Why does all of this matter, especially for those who don't follow the latest news from the comic book world? It matters because heroes help shape our culture, whether we partake in their stories or not. As the new Captain America, "Sam believes 'we need new heroes, ones suited for the times we're in,'" writes Daniel Chin. "Someone who can fight for the good guys, while also understanding that the good guys have plenty of progress to make themselves." What we define as a heroic or worthwhile story has an impact on how we live—and how we hope.[5]

Reflect

React to the difference between conservative and progressive stories and where we see hope reflected in each.

Practice

Think about the recent media you've consumed: books, TV, or movies. Do you see a pattern of one kind of narrative over another? Where do you see hope lurking in these stories?

Shifting the Point of View

~~~~~~

IN SUZANNE COLLINS's dystopian novel *The Hunger Games,* a group of young people are chosen to fight to the death against their fellow "tributes" in a specially designed arena for the entertainment of the decadent and corrupt Capitol. The Games are a means of social control, keeping the surrounding districts cowed by requiring them to sacrifice their sons and daughters in a grotesque yearly ritual. Katniss Everdeen is the protagonist in Collins's trilogy. She begins the story as a tribute from the lowly District 12, volunteering to take the place of her younger sister Prim, who is chosen by lottery.

The male tribute from District 12 is a boy Katniss's age named Peeta Mellark. The two District 12 competitors have a conversation as they prepare to enter the arena the next day. Peeta says, "I want to die as myself. I don't want them to change me in there. Turn me into some kind of monster I'm not."

Katniss scoffs at his naivete: "Who cares?" she asks. It seems foolish to dwell on such things, pawns as they are in the Capitol's sick machinations.[1]

But Peeta knows: in dark times, we may not prevail, but we can remain faithful to the values and principles we hold dear. We can keep the faith. *Who will we be in this world? What story will we write?* No matter how dire our circumstances, those questions still shine through. As Viktor Frankl realized in the death camps during the Holocaust: "Everything can be taken from a man or a woman but one thing: the last of human freedoms to choose one's attitude in any given set of circumstances, to choose one's own way."[2]

Katniss says she doesn't understand Peeta's desire to die "as himself." But her behavior shows that she understands all too well because she refuses to compromise key aspects of her own humanity. In the arena, Katniss befriends a fellow tribute named Rue, who later dies. Katniss commemorates her life by gathering white flowers and placing them around Rue's head, in her arms, and around the body. She does this in memory of her friend, in recognition of her humanity, her worth—not just as a pawn in the Capitol's power games but as a person. There's a dignity that can never be taken away.

At this point, the narrative takes an interesting turn, depending on whether you're reading the book or watching the film adaptation. The book is told from Katniss's point of view and hers alone. In the book's version of events, Katniss honors Rue for her own reasons. She doesn't see and can't know in the moment the effect her actions have on others.

But her actions do have an effect.

What the movie makes clear is that the people of Rue's district see the makeshift funeral unfold in real time. The grief and hurt break them open, and a riot ensues. A revolution has begun against the Capitol.

As a former English major, I could pontificate at length on the merits of the book's first-person limited point of view (we see everything through Katniss's eyes alone) versus the movie's third-person omniscient storytelling (we see the broader picture, including events Katniss can't know). As a seeker of hope though, I'm left to ruminate on how these two points of view dance with one another.

It's a heady thing when first person collides with third person—when we confront the impact we have on others, and others on us. I remember preaching a sermon early in my ministry about stepping out in faith and courage. Some weeks later, a woman in the congregation told me she'd finally decided to relocate to another state, something she'd been thinking about doing for years but finally dared to do it, thanks in part to my words from the pulpit.

Here's a secret among pastors: we're often preaching to ourselves first—the good news we desperately need to hear. I was stunned, and a bit distressed, that my words would inspire actual phone calls to a realtor and the U-Haul place. I wanted to say, "Oh my goodness, no. I mean . . . I'm just *talking* up there." But isn't this how it works? I've taken my own courageous steps thanks to inspiration from others. Your action begets my reaction begets someone else's. We're all living in our own first-person stories. But our stories intersect one another's in ways we both can and can't see. Some of these intersections lead to calamity—we've seen plenty of that throughout history. But sometimes, occasionally, hope is kindled too.

Reflect

Consider the ways that your individual story has intersected with communal ones. Reflect on the ways gender, race, class, and identity have played a role.

Practice

Write a letter to someone whose life inspired you to take courageous action. Thank them for the encouragement.

OUR FAMILY REWATCHES the movie *Frozen II* on a semi-frequent ba-
sis, and each time I'm bowled over by the deep wisdom in Anna's song,
"The Next Right Thing." At that point in the story, Princess Anna is as
low as she's ever been—alone and in a literal cave. She is ready to give
in to despair. She's ready to give up. And yet a tiny voice murmurs in
her soul: "hope is gone, but you must go on." She finds her way out of a
literal dark hole by breaking it down to "this next breath, this next step,
this next choice."[1]

I'm struck every time by how unflinching the song is. Hope doesn't
triumphantly return in the final verse. (So much for the stereotypically
chipper Disney chorus!) Yes, Anna stumbles into what she must do, step
by step. But she takes these actions without expectation of success: "it's
clear that everything will never be the same again" she sings—and that's
the climax of the song!

When grief presses down on us—when hope feels elusive—we can
get stuck in a seemingly interminable *now*. Yet something propels Anna
to act. What is it? It's agency. It's determination. It's one stubborn move
at a time that keeps the story going. Sometimes, the next right thing
helps us feel hope again. Other times, we realize that maybe we can move
forward without that feeling.

In her book *How to Lead When You Don't Know Where You're Going*,
Susan Beaumont expands on the wisdom we hear in Anna's song. Beaumont writes about times of transition and threshold, known as limin-

ality. She doesn't provide a road map for these in-between moments. Instead she lifts up a series of practices, conversations, and areas of focus. What questions should we ask ourselves? What do we need to be paying attention to?

A favorite passage in the book deals with "proximate purpose," a term coined by organizational consultant Gil Rendle. In Beaumont's words: "Proximate purpose [is] the next appropriate piece of work. . . . A proximate purpose will encourage people to walk to the end of the beam of light cast by the flashlight they are holding, in order to cast the beam just a little further, to see an additional fragment of the beam ahead."

Beaumont and Rendle make a distinction between proximate purpose and aspirational purpose: "In liminal seasons, when we can't visualize our destination, proximate purpose is more useful than aspirational purpose. Clarity of focus about our next few steps is more important than a fuzzy picture of an unrecognizable destination."[2]

I've written elsewhere about how an improvisational mindset can help us get unstuck. We don't need to know our destination in order to take a step, see what gets revealed, and then take another. Improvisation also keeps us from being too tied to success and progress. As T. S. Eliot said, "For us, there is only the trying. The rest is not our business." It's this mindset that helps Anna find her way out of the cave and into her intermediate goal, her proximate purpose.

Maybe Jesus would back me up on this. "Do not worry about your life," he says, "what you will eat or what you will wear. Consider the lilies of the field and the birds of the air. They do not sow or reap, and yet God takes care of them" (Matt. 6:25–26).

As much as I like a good plan, my day-to-day existence is usually too chaotic for anything but proximate, just-in-time living. I'm comforted that Jesus sanctions this approach as faithful, not deficient. That doesn't mean we do not plan. Nor are we passive and wait for things to come to us. But our tomorrows are built out of countless imperfect todays. We can't wait for everything to be ideal before we act.

A proximate purpose keeps us from flailing and gives intention to our fumbling, imperfect steps. And because it's a more immediate goal, it can provide more immediate clarity. Recently a coaching client read aloud her organization's mission statement, and we marveled at how remote and inapt it sounded given the chaos of our current time. It might as well have been written in middle English; it was all aspirational purpose, and in the turmoil of the current moment, she had no idea what to even do with it. In tumultuous times, the questions might be: *Where is the flashlight beam pointing? What is our current reason for being? How are we called to minimize suffering and embody grace in this season?* These questions are rightsized for the moment, but they also have a sense of urgency. They point us somewhere close and don't let us off the hook.

We're writing the story of our lives all the time, but we don't get to see too far down the road. That doesn't mean we lose hope. Rather, we're free to keep the hope bite-sized and proximate, one next right thing at a time.

Reflect

Do you have an aspirational purpose for your life? How does that aspiration lead you to live differently today?

Practice

Listen to "The Next Right Thing" from *Frozen II*. Make it the first track in a "get it done" playlist of tunes that help you get moving.

Hopeful Stories Need Tricksters

As a family of nerds, we're huge fans of the character Loki, the beloved trickster god based on Norse mythology that populates Marvel lore. Loki has been both a villain and a reluctant, not entirely trustworthy hero over the years, which is part of what makes him so beloved in our house and fun to watch.

We've seen Loki be defeated and even die multiple times during the movies, though he frequently comes back, sometimes because he's a god and isn't easily stopped, sometimes because the story needs him, and sometimes because, well, comic book stories love a good reboot. (We also know it's because Loki is a fan favorite, and the big corporation is in it for the cash. What can I say? So long as you make fun, thought-provoking stories, Marvel, take my money.)

During a poignant moment in Loki's story, when the situation seems very bleak, a character named Sylvie (sort of a variation on Loki) asks him, "Do you think what makes a Loki a Loki is that we are destined to lose?" Loki responds: "No. We may lose. Sometimes painfully. But we don't die, we survive."[1]

Tricksters exist the world over—Anansi, Coyote, Narada, Br'er Rabbit—but they're most potent in the folklore of indigenous and marginalized communities. Their function is to do what it takes to survive, win or lose.

In United States culture, competition and dominance feature heavily. Being "the world's last superpower" and "the most powerful nation in the world" are potent aspects of self-identity, accurate or not, for better and worse. During the Olympics, network news coverage trumpets the medal count compared to other countries. We love to win.

But our stories betray our true hearts. We find sports dynasties boring and root for Cinderella teams during March Madness. We love an upset and relish the underdog. We can't get enough of survival-against-the-odds storylines. These are the narratives we gravitate to. Our country may be a long way from the "young, scrappy, and hungry" revolutionaries Lin-Manuel Miranda wrote about in *Hamilton*, but that impulse is still there, which may mean there's still hope for us.

The trickster, the underdog, is essential for hopeful fiction. It's the tricksters that disrupt the status quo, that relentlessly fight for survival for themselves and their people. Tricksters are the ants in the pants of hope.

While many of us appreciate the trickster, those who have privilege need to acknowledge that tricksters are often fighting to prevail against the likes of us. Ethicist Miguel de la Torre finds inspiration from the trickster, particularly the image of the *joderon*, a figure whose name loosely (and euphemistically) translates to "one who screws with the powers that be." A *joderon* "strategically becomes a royal pain in the ass, purposely causes trouble, constantly disrupts the established norm . . . and audaciously refuses to stay in his or her assigned place. . . . To *joder* is to overturn traditional tables." De la Torre emphasizes that true *joderones* are animated not by vengeance or a desire to "stick it to the man." Rather, to *joder* is to commit an act of love toward one's oppressors, compelling them to live up to their expressed ideals, and hopefully, to lead them to their own salvation and conversion.[2]

De la Torre sees the spirit of *joderon* among the Young Lords, a Puerto Rican gang in New York City in the 1960s. Members of their community had complained endlessly to the city because their garbage wasn't being picked up on the prearranged schedule. So the Young Lords and other neighbors packed up the trash and trucked it to an area of New York where it could not be ignored—where "all the rich white folks were trying to get out of town," as one remembers—and set the trash on fire.

The police showed up, of course. But the newspapers showed up too. They took pictures and reported the story. And the garbage started getting picked up on its regular schedule.[3]

"We may lose. Sometimes painfully. But we don't die. We survive." A hopeful story will have its share of false starts and setbacks. With any luck, it will have the spirit of the trickster as well, afflicting the comfortable, disturbing the peace, and refusing to give up and give in.

Reflect

"It's the tricksters that disrupt the status quo, that relentlessly fight for survival for themselves and their people." React to this statement.

Practice

Who are the *joderones* in your community that are agitating against oppressive structures for the sake of liberation? How might you ally with them?

Rethinking (Happy) Endings

WHEN GEORGE FLOYD was killed by police in Minneapolis, people of all races and backgrounds took to the streets. Businesses issued statements and invested in staff to address diversity, equity, and inclusion. Books about racism flew off the shelves. And a large contingent of White people began antiracism work for the first time.

Over time, a lot of the zeal faded. Some people lost motivation, the immediate needs of their lives taking over. For others, the work proved too destabilizing to the foundational stories on which they'd based their lives. Some have stuck with the task, realizing it's the work of a lifetime. But many of us still secretly hold out hope for the three-step plan, the antiracist job description, the definitive set of actions that, once checked off, will fix everything. But it's as true of antiracism work as it is of any justice work—anything worth doing will not be completed quickly and easily. There is no end point.

In his book *The Infinite Game*, Simon Sinek makes a distinction between finite and infinite games. A finite game has set players, well-articulated rules, and a specific objective. Infinite games have a variety of players, each with different objectives, and there's no definitive conclusion; the goal is to keep playing. Baseball is a finite game. Life is an infinite game. Sinek argues that much of business is played like a finite game, with winners and losers, successes and failures. But business is actually an infinite game, requiring an abundant, open-ended mindset. Finite-minded organizations jockey with one another for a sliver of a prebaked pie. Infinite-minded organizations learn how to bake additional pies.[1]

108

Justice work is an infinite game. The goal is to keep the game going, to make the world better so we can keep making the world better.

In the hours before Jesus's arrest and crucifixion, an unnamed woman comes and anoints his head with expensive oil. His disciples scoff at the woman's extravagance; after all, the oil could have been sold and the proceeds used to help those in need. Jesus praises the woman for doing a beautiful thing for him and chastises the naysayers, saying, "you always have the poor with you . . . but you will not always have me." The verse has vexed justice-hearted people for centuries. But Jesus isn't throwing up his hands and saying that poverty is inevitable, so what's the point. He's saying, "You'll never not have work to do, so plan accordingly." He was describing the infinite game. Each victory opens a new set of opportunities. A conclusion to one story sets us up for a sequel.

Many of us are suckers for a good ending. I love the photos of celebrations at the end of World War II: the cheering in the streets, the skies awash with ticker tape, the embrace of friends and strangers alike. We crave catharsis and closure.

But few chapters of our lives end so definitively. I have friends who've been through chemotherapy who get to ring a bell after their final treatment. What a beautiful end! But it's not really the end. There are still residual effects and worry. The medication, the miraculous toxic medication, is still in the system, hopefully killing the cancer and wreaking as little havoc on the rest of the body as possible.

There may not ever be an ending, let alone a happy one. So much of our lives takes place *in medias res*—in the midst of things.

Six months into Caroline's depressive episode, when things were stable and slowly improving, I enlisted a few family members to write letters on the six-month anniversary of the day our kid reached out and said, "I can't carry this around anymore. I'm hurting."

A wise friend with mental-health training warned me against this. Perhaps this milestone was important for me, but it may not be for my daughter, he argued. Perhaps I was imposing meaning on an event that wasn't there.

I heard the concern but rationalized that as a religious person, I believe in the power of marking time, of commemorating milestones along the road. So much of life is beyond our control, but ritual can help give shape to our stories.

When Caroline crashed again later that year, worse than before, I understood the wisdom behind my friend's caution. Despite the milestone, our daughter hadn't been truly "better," except in the sense of having a lot of infrastructure in place when the depression flared up even worse. When I heard a little voice in my head say, "But we had a ritual!" I realized I'd made a bargain with the universe without even realizing it: that if I structured the story a specific way, I could control it. If we wrote letters and offered words of blessing and courage, it would all be behind us. Six months. Done and done.

But I kissed a stranger in the middle of Times Square. Doesn't that mean we won the war?

I'm still finding my way in this, and I'm still a fan of milestones. During the COVID-19 quarantine, our family marked day fifty, day one hundred, day two hundred, and so on, not as endings, but as acknowledgments of what we'd survived thus far. (Also, any excuse to have cake . . .) I have to take care not to impose an order that isn't there. But milestones do matter. They reveal moments of resilience. They're like cairns, those piles of stones along a hiking path that say *I was here. I went by this way.*

Lord of the Rings fans poke affectionate fun at the fact that the final movie of the early-2000s trilogy has several endings. Closure is tough for a three-film, eleven-hour saga, it turns out. One of my favorite scenes is short and understated. It's of the four main hobbits back in their sweet, unassuming village, in a local pub, after their harrowing adventure ends. (The movie trilogy begins the series at a Hobbit party, so we've seen how festive these events can be, with fireworks, food, and tall tales for the children.)

Despite the merriment all around them, there is no clinking of mugs for our heroes, no jubilant slapping on the back, no expressions of joy. Instead they sip quietly on their drinks amid the din all around them. They give each other knowing looks. They seem older, weathered from the ordeal. If there's joy, it's a knowing, subdued kind.

In a world filled with great sorrow as well as great delight, sometimes a jubilant sense of closure is out of reach. But a quiet toast with friends before the next adventure begins? That we can do.

In his essay "Losing the War," Lee Sandlin argues that once World War II ended, many people stopped talking about it, with many of the most personal details lost to time:

> But there is another and simpler reason the war has been forgotten: people wanted to forget it. It had gone on for so many years, had destroyed so much, had killed so many—most U.S. casualties were in the final year of fighting. When it came to an end, people were glad to be rid of everything about it. That was what surprised commentators about the public reaction in America and Europe when the news broke that Germany and then Japan had at last surrendered. In the wild celebrations that followed nobody crowed, "Our enemies are destroyed." Nobody even yelled, "We've won." What they all said instead was, "The war is over."[2]

This is the kind of hope that lives *in medias res*. If there's an end, it's only a provisional end. The end of a chapter, the pause before something new begins and we pick up the work once more. That's not a reason to lose hope; it's an invitation to see hope lurking even in the murky midst of things.

Reflect

Consider what it means to live *in medias res*. Do we ever see the end of the story? How does that open-endedness facilitate hope? How does it hinder it?

Practice

Are there aspects of your life that you've been treating as finite games? What would need to shift in order to see them as infinite ones?

5

The Practice of Hope

"The very least you can do in your life is figure out what you hope for," writes Barbara Kingsolver. "And the most you can do is live inside that hope."[1]

We've unlearned some things about hope; we've explored what it is and where to find it; and we've found our way into hope as a narrative.

What do we do with hope? How do we live inside of it?

Here are some places to start.

The Practice of Pointing the Compass

WHEN DIRE NEWS BREAKS, and social media teems with anxiety and despair, I have a writer I consult for analysis, perspective, and most importantly, a palpable lowering of temperature. His work is often some variation on "Here's another way to look at this. Yes, it may turn out as awful as 'they' say. Or it may not be that bad, and here's why."

A mutual friend also reads this particular writer, though not as regularly, and she asked me whether I'd found his calm analysis to prove correct over time. She wanted to know his "track record."

At first, I was brought up short—I hadn't thought to keep tabs on his accuracy. But then I realized, for me the question is irrelevant because he's not trying to predict the future. What he's doing is orienting himself, and his readers, in the direction of what's good, what's possible. When the chattering classes on cable and Twitter see the sky as definitively falling, he sees the same data but points in the direction of potential, to give people somewhere to go.

This writer is fond of saying that hope is an ethic. It's less important to me that he's proved correct in the details. What matters to me is a vision of justice and goodness that inspires us to act. A hopeful orientation of the spirit is one that I desperately need.

This approach is countercultural, especially on the Internet, where detached fatalism often rules the day. A friend I love dearly, when faced with the latest headline of absurdity, is a master of the form. "That's it."

"We're screwed." "Nothing matters anymore." It is becoming cool to give up.

It cannot become cool to give up. Or if it does, count me out. (Although honestly, I'm in my 50s now; that ship sailed a long time ago.) As podcaster and former speechwriter Jon Lovett has said, "Being too cynical and pleasantly surprised is not more sophisticated than being too idealistic and disappointed."

As is probably evident in the pages of this book, running is an important part of my life. It's my recreation and self-medication, in addition to being a joy and a way to care for my physical health. But there are plenty of times when I just don't wanna. I know I can, and I'll feel better when I do, but the weight of inertia is heavy.

In those cases, I have a phrase I use. I say to myself, out loud if necessary, "MaryAnn, the patriarchy wants you lazy on this couch."

It always, always works.

It's embarrassing to admit this. I can't quite believe I'm sharing it in print. (I told you I didn't care about being cool.) I know "the patriarchy" doesn't care whether a middle-aged lady gets her hill repeats done. But whether anyone's looking or not, getting up, taking care of myself, and staying strong is a matter of orientation, with hope as an ethic. (When I write about running, I'm always talking about more than running.)

Writing on Facebook, Will Stenberg concludes a lengthy rant with this:

> When we say "we're f***ed" we roll over. We defeat ourselves. Don't do that . . . we are in a fight. It sucks. It's hard. People are suffering. The earth is suffering. It will get worse. . . . Look at history. People have been so much more f***ed than us, and won. If you truly believe we are finished, but I'm sorry, but you were the first to fall. I don't want to see you do that, if only for the selfish reason that we need you.[1]

It may be as bad as it looks. The forces of injustice, of cruelty, of ignorance, of division—what the apostle Paul called the powers and principalities—may have the upper hand. They may in fact prevail. As

Miguel de la Torre says, the powers are always ten steps ahead of those of who care about justice work.[2] Still, we orient ourselves, map in hand, compass trained on hope.

Reflect

React to the idea of hope as an orientation rather than a goal or destination.

Practice

The next time you consume the news (whether through the Internet, TV, or a newspaper), notice when you feel yourself slipping into despair. What would it take to keep your compass trained on hope?

MY PARTICULAR BRANCH of Christianity doesn't have a pope or bishops handing down decisions for the rest of the church. What we have, for better and worse, is one another. We are self-governing, which looks like a variety of democratically elected leaders at multiple levels of governance and culminates in a subset of these leaders gathering every two years in a national meeting called the General Assembly.

Imagine hundreds of people in an over-airconditioned conference center, decked out in lanyards and comfortable shoes, gathering in committees, hearing reports, taking stands yea and nay, and hopefully, exemplifying the wisdom of the crowd, the conviction that together we see much more truth than any single one of us can.

GA is equal parts heartening and mind-numbing. For every inspiring testimony of a group doing bold justice-building work, family-reunion-style conversation over dinner or in the exhibit hall, or surprising moment of grace, there are late nights of wordsmithing, tedious parliamentary maneuvers ("having been perfected as a motion, shall the substitute motion become the main motion?"), and politicking by interest groups.

I was attending one of these GA meetings some years ago when the family separation policy at the US border came to full light.

The crisis at the border shined a harsh light on some of the picayune insider decisions being made about the church's governance and structure. Who could possibly care about non-geographic synods or restructuring the denomination's central office? It was surreal to observe committee meetings and have conversations in hotel lobbies and a fancy convention hall, knowing there were children along our southern border who had no idea when or whether they would see their parents again.

I was grateful to be around people who were mostly as pained and appalled as I felt. Immigration is a tough, tangled issue, befuddling count-less presidential administrations regardless of party. But as a Christian, it's hard to see much gray area in taking children from their parents and putting them up in warehouses. Jesus said in Matthew 25, "that which you did to the least of these, you did to me." And he didn't stutter.

The prevailing temptation, then and now, is numbness. The onslaught of bad news often feels unrelenting, and it's hard to even figure out what's accurate, let alone what to do about it. And the actions of an informed citizen—writing a letter, casting a vote—feel so paltry in the wake of political forces that are much bigger than all of us.

One day, we took a break from the committee meetings and plenary sessions to march en masse to the city's justice center, carrying with us $47,000 to bail some thirty-six people out of jail. These were folks who were simply awaiting trial, but because they lacked the funds to post bail, they were languishing in the meantime, away from partners, children, jobs, and communities.

It was inspiring to put faith into action, to do something public and specific to "set captives free." It also felt like not nearly enough to address the world's wounds, as news broke on our phones and TVs of so-called tender age shelters for infants and toddlers along the border.

The week before, I'd heard an interview with Lin-Manuel Miranda and Thomas Kail, the creative team behind the musical *Hamilton*. They talked about the early days of working on the musical—writing, edit-ing, and refining it—and how overwhelming it seemed. They adopted a motto, co-opted from Jerome Robbins when *Fiddler on the Roof* was in previews in Detroit. Things were not going well for the fledgling produc-tion. Kail says: "There's this moment when Fiddler is really struggling, and Austin Pendleton, a young actor at this point, said, 'What are we going to do?' and Robbins said, 'Ten things a day.'"

"Just do the thing," Kail continues. "Do the stuff that's in front of you: 'What can we accomplish today?' We would come in after a show, and Lin and I would talk to each other . . . and we'd say OK, what can we accomplish at this time. And you just start chipping away."[1]

Even our act of posting bail, singular as it was, was the result of a "ten things" mindset. Once the location of the General Assembly was set, church officials began working with organizers and community leaders, building relationships, learning the needs of the community, and discerning how the Presbyterian Church (USA) might support them. Step by step, they found their way into an action that, while being a specific action on a specific day, will become part of the deeper work of advocacy around criminal-justice reform.[2]

In my experience coaching leaders, many clients know where they want to go, but they're immobilized by the tremendous size of the task. So we work together on the principle of "ten things a day"—small, bite-sized pieces that slowly but surely move us forward. It's a way of staying present to today's work instead of tomorrow's results, which we can never control. We live in chaotic, perilous times. Regardless of our particular convictions and beliefs, numbing out is a luxury we cannot afford. No one can do everything, but everyone can do something. At times, the "something" is to pull back and rest—but always in the service of a deeper engagement, one small act at a time.

Reflect

We all numb out from time to time. What kinds of circumstances tempt you to do so? What are some of your go-to numbing behaviors?

Practice

Practice the art of ten things. When you feel overwhelmed or uncertain, or are tempted to tune out, make a list of tiny behaviors that could move you forward with purpose. If they still feel too hard to complete, make them even smaller.

The Practice of Finding What's Stable

~~~~~~

OUR HOUSE IS LOCATED on a small lake, where I've been learning to paddleboard. I'd always heard it was a good activity for one's core fitness, but I had no idea. I'm never as sore as I am after going out for a paddle, whether sitting (hello arms and back), kneeling (hello quads), or standing (hello everything).

But the biggest challenge is balance. For years I've watched people paddle around, all elegant silhouettes against sparkling waters, and marveled at how graceful they looked. I imagined I would have that same elegance on the board.

Instead, I get on it and wobble, wobble, wobble. I haven't fallen in, but I probably will eventually. I'm OK with that, even as I work to become more confident on the board and fluid in my motions.

Here's the thing I have to remember:

The paddleboard is stable.

Because it's so wide, it would take a lot for it to flip over, or even tip me over. And our lake doesn't allow large motors, so I don't have to worry about any large wakes coming along.

The paddleboard is stable.

It's *me* that's wobbly.

You'd think that wouldn't be much comfort—if I go into the drink, does it really matter why?—but it makes all the difference. I may waver and I may fall, but I don't need to worry about the paddleboard making that happen. I can trust what's under my feet.

Every time I'm out on the board lately, that is my mantra: *The pad-dleboard is stable. The paddleboard is stable.* And knowing that helps keep me stable and strong.

I once heard a rabbi talk about different names for God in scripture and in the Jewish tradition. The most *common* name for God in scripture is "Elohim," which means the "one who is the object of reverence." Perhaps the most *important* name is the one people pronounce as "Yahweh" ("I am who I am"). But many believe that the earliest name for God is pronounced "ha-makom."

"Ha-makom" means "the Place."

The earliest name for God is the Place! Remarkable. Before we began hanging a bunch of theological attributes on God, God was simply a place—*the* place. Before God was ever a Who, God was a Where.

Whether it's a pandemic, or economic uncertainty, or the profound messy reckoning of our country's legacy of racism and White supremacy, the ground is shifting under our feet. In fact, we're not really on solid earth at all. We're out on the water, the water is a-troubled, and our knees are shaking.

It's awkward and unsettling to wobble. And my place in life means my "paddleboard" is wide thanks in part to a heap of privilege. It's easy to trust that the board is stable when it always has come through for us. The question is available to anyone, however: What is stable in my life right now? What can be trusted?

There are times when the answer is alarmingly small. The board may be narrow. But maybe it's enough for the moment. A friend who works in drug abuse counseling, in recovery herself, has seen firsthand the life-saving power of "just for today." *Don't worry about not using for the rest of your life,* she tells those she counsels. *Focus on making it through the workday. Then focus on the drive home. Then focus on making it to bedtime.* The task becomes grounded in the moment, because the moment has all the stability we can muster—all that's needed.

Even amid the wobbliness, I believe in ha-makom, a great trust-worthy stability undergirding all things, or what Paul Tillich called the Ground of All Being. Your conception of the cosmic paddleboard may differ—Martin Luther King's arc of the moral universe, the goodness within humanity, love itself. It may not be a deity at all. So be it. Whatever it is, when we start to waver and shake, we can pause and take a moment to feel what's reliably under our feet.

Reflect

An early name for God is "the Place." React to this image. What does it open up for you? If your belief system doesn't include a supreme being, where do you find your grounding when you're at your best?

Practice

When you feel yourself starting to waver or lose hope, take a minute to close your eyes, sit with your feet flat on the ground, breathe, and feel the earth beneath your feet. Find a mantra or short phrase that can help you remember what's stable and reliable in your life.

The Practice of Surviving the Winter

~~~~~~

DURING THE FIRST FALL of the pandemic, I began to hear public health officials issue warnings about a very long and grim winter. The phrase "grim winter" came up again and again, eventually leading me to reread Laura Ingalls Wilder's classic children's book, *The Long Winter*, which could also have been called *The Grim Winter.* In it she tells the story of her family and the other residents of De Smet, South Dakota, describing in harrowing detail how they survived (barely) during seven months of brutal winter. Blizzards relentlessly pelted the town, the train got stuck before supplies could reach them, and food stores got perilously low. Laura and her family subsisted on brown bread, potatoes, and tea. Even Pa, ever the source of twinkle-eyed positivity in Wilder's books, was sorely tested, and reading the book as a parent, it took my breath away to imagine the stress of keeping things normal while worrying sick that your children wouldn't live to see the spring.

Reading it, I saw once again how hope transcends optimism; Pa's positive attitude falls short at a couple of key moments. Rather, hope is an alignment toward the next right action, even in dire circumstances we cannot control. As Vaclav Havel said, "Hope is not prognostication. It is an orientation of the spirit."[1]

Wilder spends little time reflecting on the existential dread of their situation, aside from a few alarming moments when it was hard to even think clearly due to malnutrition. The gift of children's books is that they keep things very concrete, and *The Long Winter* offers a few tangible suggestions for enduring our own grim times.

Tie a lifeline. The blizzard gets so thick and the wind so fierce that even the short distance from the house to the barn is too far to go without a guide; one could easily lose their way and stumble into the open prairie, never to be found again. So Pa runs a rope between the two structures, which allows him, hand over hand, to travel safely.

When the wind howls and the gloom descends, we need a lifeline, which could be anything:

A person.

A ritual.

A song.

A location.

A book.

A memory.

A gameplan.

Twist hay. The family runs out of firewood, so Pa Ingalls twists small bits of hay into tight bundles to burn, and later teaches Laura the grueling, tedious work. I think about how much slower it must have been for Pa in the beginning, taking time to instruct his young daughter, stopping, correcting her technique, and starting again. Once she learns, she helps build up their supply of fuel, but perhaps as important, Pa gives her agency to be a part of her family's survival.

Still, I imagined how dry and raw their hands must have gotten, and how mind-numbing the task had to be. Yet it must be done. Here's to all the unglamorous elements of basic survival we undertake. They are building blocks of hope.

Create light. One of my favorite scenes of the book is when Ma Ingalls creates a button lamp out of a scrap of cloth, a coat button, and some axle grease. It doesn't provide much light, but it is enough. Pa exclaims, "You're a wonder, Caroline," and I have to think that he's responding not only to the glow from the small flame but to his wife's ingenuity, which brings a joy of its own.[2]

A while back, some neighbors brought us a few homemade cinnamon rolls in a plastic to-go container, the kind you might get from a restaurant. We returned it, filled with some cookies. A few days later, we got the container back with a slab of coffee cake. Since then, this container has bounced between the two homes, like a message in a bottle but in carb form. It gladdens my heart to wonder how long we can keep it going. It's been a small bit of light in an often-gloomy world.

Tie a lifeline. Twist hay. Make light. With a few simple practices, hope remains alive.

Reflect

What tangible actions help you get through the "winter"?

Practice

This section offers three possible practices: tying a lifeline, twisting hay, and creating light. Which one resonates with you right now? How can you help yourself remember to practice it when things get tough?

The Practice of Going Back to Basics

IT HAD BEEN A LONG RUN in the warm soup of the Virginia summer, and I was really struggling. As I mentally thumbed through my list of favorite mantras and slogans, I remembered something I'd heard on a running podcast earlier that week:

> Beginning runners focus on the pain.
> Intermediate runners focus on the mileage.
> Advanced runners focus on form.

It's been true for me. When I first started running more than a decade ago and the going got tough, all I could think about was my burning lungs or stinging quads. (Pro-tip: focusing on the pain is not a good recipe for endurance.)

As I gained more experience on my feet—as an intermediate runner—I would focus on the miles: how far I'd come, how far I still had to go. If I was feeling good, that could be motivating: *More than halfway through ... two-thirds done ... just a mile to go!* If things were going poorly, however, it was a motivation-killer: *You still have seven miles. You'll never make it. Loser!* Focusing on the mileage can be brutal in a race, especially if you're a middle-of-the-pack runner like me: *Lots of people have already finished, and you still have miles to go.*

I don't know whether I qualify as an advanced runner, but that day, struggling in the soup, I decided not to think about the pain, or where I was in my workout, but to focus on form. *Shoulders back and down. Torso tall. Quick feet. Easy breath. Arms bent at 90 degrees.*

The miles were still a tough effort, but I focused on myself and the countless small adjustments that would make my running more efficient and the remaining miles more bearable. It was a comfort to control what I could control.

When we're in the midst of deep adversity, or even just an unexpected detour, what do we do? Do we fixate on the pain and negativity until that's all we can see? Do we fret over external factors beyond our control? Or do we turn inward, breathe deeply, and focus on what we can change—namely, our own response?

Hope is built on this—not on romantic notions or lofty goals but on keeping our form in tiptop shape, so we can be of best service to ourselves, our loved ones, and the world.

Pick an issue, any issue. If we live in this world long enough, we'll have ample opportunity to have our hearts broken by it. With every school shooting, I think of my kids: one was in high school the same year of Parkland; another is the age of the Sandy Hook kids, a reminder in my home of how old those children would be now.

To focus on the pain to the exclusion of all else is beginner's mind; we will burn to a crisp. (I must also check myself, as a White person of privilege, not to insulate myself from the pain that afflicts others as a matter of course.)

It's also understandable, like the intermediate runner, to focus on the miles, to look around at our culture of violence, the sorry state of the debate over gun safety, the dearth of mental health resources for people in need, or all of the above. To wonder why the United States has such a shameful track record compared to other developed nations, and whether any change is possible. I'll be honest; I don't see much reason to hope for progress right now.

What, then, is left? To focus on form. To care for myself and the people around me. To look inward and make sure I am acting with the most integrity, wisdom, and compassion. To tend to my breathing. To do what's mine to do. In my case, that may mean giving money and writing letters and making phone calls to Congress, and also showing up to work each day, and reading nourishing books, and eating food that's good for me and for the earth so I'm around and kicking as long as possible.

To focus on form means to "run with perseverance the race that is set before us," as the author of the book of Hebrews wrote to the early church so long ago (12:1). I wish the terrain were different—less treacherous, less painful for body and soul. But the race is ours to run nonetheless, as well as we possibly can.

Reflect

When the going gets tough, where do you put your focus? How does that focus help you? How does it hinder?

Practice

Runners practice running with proper form—so should we. What postures, practices, or habits help your life "run" smoothly and with ease? Pick one this week and focus on it.

MY KIDS USED TO HOST Harry Potter movie marathons for their friends in the summer. To keep the task manageable, they would choose their favorite few films (out of the eight total) and invite friends over for themed food, decorations, and fun.

During a recent one, I happened to catch what is probably my favorite moment from the entire series, in *Harry Potter and the Prisoner of Azkaban*. Near the end of the story, at a moment of extreme peril, Harry looks into the distance and sees what he thinks is his deceased father casting a spell that helps save Harry's life.

Through the quirks of time travel, he and his friend Hermione are later able to go back to that same spot where Harry thought his father appeared. They find a good vantage point from which to watch, where Harry crouches with anticipation of his father's arrival. He watches, as if viewing a play, as a group of sinister wraiths called dementors swirls over him and his godfather, Sirius Black. (Yes, there are "two" Harry Potters, one from the future, observing the scene and one in the present. It's time travel; don't try to figure it out.)

As Future Harry waits for a glimpse of his father, he watches Sirius's life (and his own) slipping away under the dementors' attack, and he waits. *Any minute now. My father will come. He will save the day.*

Finally Hermione says quietly, "Harry. Nobody's coming." And that's when Harry realizes—there will be no hero galloping to the rescue. Present Harry had seen himself—Future Harry—casting the spell. It was up to him. So he steps up and conjures the life-saving patronus, a spell he'd been struggling with for a year.

He explains to Hermione later in the story, he knew he could do it, because, well, he'd already done it. (Time travel.)[1]

But I believe he also knew he could do it, because *he had to do it.* There was no other option.

Maybe for you, it's the scourge of racism, sexism, homophobia, or nativism. Perhaps it's the devastation of climate change, already on our doorstep with rampant fires and violent hurricanes. Or perhaps the wistfulness is more localized—broken relationships, fear and uncertainty, sadness that things aren't the way they should be.

Let me whisper this, like Hermione. Nobody's coming. It's up to us, whatever the "it" might be. So we curse the gloom and cast our spell, whatever that looks like. But we cannot wait for someone else. We're it. For those of us who identify as Christian, Teresa of Avila nuances this point even further:

> Christ has no body but yours,
> No hands, no feet on earth but yours,
> Yours are the eyes with which he looks
> Compassion on this world,
> Yours are the feet with which he walks to do good.[2]

But like Harry, we know that we have the strength to survive these terrible times, because people just like us have done hard things before, and we don't do it alone. We all step up and conjure our patronuses as best we can.

Many years ago, my colleague the late Jim Atwood received a writing award in our denomination. Jim spent some thirty years writing and advocating for more sensible gun laws; it was his life's work. In his acceptance speech, he talked about the parable of the talents, the story told by Jesus in which a landowner gives three servants varying amounts of money, called talents.

Jim looked around him and saw people he considered to have outsized talents and abilities and kept waiting for one of them to lend their gifts to the issue of gun violence. *Their writing gifts are so much greater than mine,* he thought. *They have a larger audience, more influence.* He waited and waited and finally realized that he needed to stop waiting for someone else to pick up the cause that he felt so convicted about.

He stepped out in faith and cast his spell. He used his talent to say what he believed and to be a voice of conscience in the church and beyond.

Nobody's coming.

Just Harry.

Just Jim.

Just you and me.

Reflect

"It's up to us, whatever the 'it' might be. . . . We cannot wait for someone else. We're it." React to this statement.

Practice

For the next week, pay attention to how you talk about the big and small challenges facing our world in general and your community in particular. Notice when you're tempted to blame or put the responsibility elsewhere. What part might you play?

The Practice of the Big Three

IT'S EASY TO LOSE HEART and feel disconnected from hope, especially if you follow the news. Sometimes I manage to feel hopeful, even when the pain in the world feels overwhelming. Other times, life seems relatively OK, and yet I struggle with despair. Why the mismatch?

After a lot of discernment, I've realized that my ability to access hope boils down to the presence, or absence, of three basic elements. I offer them here, in a section on practice, because when I'm wrung out, having some areas of focus can help. Feel free to borrow these, adapt them, or be inspired to make your own list.

My first essential for hope is *beauty.*

When I'm neglecting beauty, I'm disconnected from the natural world, and/or from art, music, or story—forces that were here before me and will be here after me.

Some years ago, the pastor and writer Samuel Wells found himself in one of those "what would you put on your tombstone" types of conversations. He recalls blurting out an idea that arrived fully formed, one of those thoughts he didn't know he had until he heard it in his own voice:

> If it can't be happy, make it beautiful.

"All these years later," he wrote in a recent article, "I haven't changed my mind."[1] The phrase has been a guiding principle for his ministry, particularly when memorializing the deceased. Amid the sadness, there is beauty, and that beauty provides comfort. Inspiration. Fuel. Connection.

On one of the saddest days of my kid's depression, when no amount of cajoling, encouraging, or (let's face it) bribery could get Caroline out of bed to go to school, I threw up my hands and said, "Forget it. We're going on a field trip." We ended up at ARTECHOUSE, a small museum in DC that includes immersive and interactive floor-to-ceiling digital murals. We waved our arms and watched digital cherry blossoms float on the wind. We passed through rooms outfitted with augmented reality images we accessed from our phones. We sipped whimsical drinks containing pop rocks and topped with cotton candy.

It wasn't a happy day. Nothing got fixed. But it was a beautiful one, and it reminded us both that when the world is bleak, artists can connect us to color, context, whimsy, and meaning.

My second essential for hope is *relationships*.

When I'm neglecting relationships, I see others as burdens or obstacles, or myself as a "doing" machine.

Studies show that when we're lonely, our cortisol (stress hormone) levels can soar to similar levels as when we're experiencing a physical attack. In his book *Lost Connections*, Johann Hari argues that in most cases, loneliness is a *precursor* to depressive symptoms, rather than a by-product.[2]

It's one of the most magical paradoxes of life, that doing something for someone else can help us feel better about ourselves—and feel better, *period*. But sometimes the despair can rob us of that kind of energy. In these moments, it's a gift to rely on others for a chat or just silent company. The Quaker writer Parker Palmer has spoken about his experiences of depression and how one particularly bleak season was made easier by a friend who would come over every day, not to talk but simply to rub his feet. Parker remembers, "Somehow he found the one place in my body, namely the soles of my feet, where I could experience some sort of connection to another human being. And the act of massaging just—in a way that I really don't have words for—kept me connected with the human race."[3]

My third essential is *action*.

When I'm neglecting action, I'm usually fretting, complaining, or yelling into the void, not doing what's mine to do. I forget my own power.

Gregory Ellison, activist and professor at Emory University, likes to quote his auntie, who'd say, "Greg, I may not be able to change the world, but I can change the three feet around me."[4]

My cousin Bess, an education professor in Florida, is a master at the small action, which she freely admits is to save her own soul as much as anything. Sometimes these actions are more substantial, like knitting a sweater for a friend's new baby. But usually it's dropping a note in the mail or putting together a simple thank-you package for her kid's teacher. It's no wonder she was recently honored by her university with an award for kindness.

None of these actions will change the world—or will they? But they certainly change the three feet around her. And that's enough.

Reflect

"If it can't be happy, make it beautiful." Explore this quote from Samuel Wells. How does it expand your ideas about hope?

Practice

This section suggests three places to put focus when hope seems low: beauty, relationships, and action. Which one feels most needed right now? Or come up with your own checklist. Find an accountability partner to help you make time and effort for this component of hope.

I'M IN LINE AT THE COFFEE SHOP, already running late before I dashed in the door. I quickly realize the person at the front counter won't be doing me any favors. He's got a list of six beverages, each with its own specific, nit-picking substitution or adaptation, which he orders with unhurried obliviousness to the people stacked up behind him. Moment by moment, my irritation grows, my internal sociologist spinning out an uncharitable theory about our supposedly narcissistic age: *Must we? Why do we need fifty different variations on coffee?* I'm staring into the middle distance, wondering whether my expression communicates annoyance or equanimity. If I'm honest, I want to convey the former but with enough of the latter to give me plausible deniability. I prepare to order a pointedly uncomplicated tea.

The man is wearing a suit. To pass the time, I find myself inventing reasons why someone would be dressed up at 8 a.m. on a Saturday morning. Laundry day and everything else is dirty? Job interview? (But then why the multiple drinks?) Stayed out all night and is on his way home to a houseful of roommates?

I finally decide he's attending a family funeral and is picking up beverages for the family of the deceased. Suddenly his niggling order takes on a different meaning. Rather than evidence of an indulgent "I must have it my way!" society, the careful details are a means for this gentleman to show care and comfort for others. And his halting manner isn't a can't-be-bothered self-centeredness but a painstaking effort to get this one thing right for people for whom everything has gone wrong.

Of course I have no idea whether he's really going to a funeral. But it doesn't matter. In a moment of improvised imagination, I'm already breathing more deeply, relaxing into the waiting just a bit, and even (could it be?) beaming a little love toward this stranger.

I've stumbled into a concept that philosopher Kwame Anthony Appiah calls "useful fictions." "There is a gap between what is true and what is useful to believe," writes Appiah.[1] Sometimes that's because the truth is too big for our minds to encompass, so we need a shorthand. Other times it's because we have a pretty good idea how something works, but it's not ironclad, so we go with what's roughly right. If I exercise and eat nutritious food, I could still fall prey to heart disease, but the odds are on my side if I take care of myself. Useful fictions aren't the same as "alternative facts"—they are grounded in reality and oriented toward the good.

In the case of slow coffee-house patrons, the truth isn't particularly complex, just unknowable. In such situations, the question becomes, who do I want to be in this scenario, and what would need to be true in order for me to be that person? And to act as if that were true. (Appiah's book, fittingly enough, is called *As If.*)

Every now and then, I remember to apply this kind of reframe, imagining the most charitable scenario. Some people do this work naturally, but my mind often wants to go to the least generous interpretation of events. So I have to work at it: a surly cashier is at the end of a long shift and has a sick child at home. A standoffish co-worker isn't rude, just extremely introverted. On a recent vacation road trip, our family was moaning over the stop-and-go traffic, and with a cringe I remembered that we, too, were someone else's traffic.

How am I doing with this practice? I get it right maybe 9 percent of the time. Here's another useful fiction: the fact that I have so far to go means it won't take much effort for me to see improvement.

In her research on courage and authenticity, Brené Brown found that the most wholehearted people believe that everyone is basically doing the best they can. Many are sheepish to admit it. "I know it sounds silly," they say, as if worrying they'd come across as naïve rubes. Brown makes clear that good boundaries are vital to wholehearted living, which keeps us from being taken advantage of by people whose "best" is bound to hurt us. And we're wise to wonder how we got to the point, culturally or educationally, where people's "best" still results in cruelty, sexism, racism, homophobia, and more.

But when we apply the frame that people are doing their best, it turns the focus around to ourselves. As one business leader put it in a workshop with Brown, after sharing a case study about an underperforming co-worker, "If he's doing the best he can, I'm a total jerk, and I need to stop harassing him and start helping him."

Brown responded, "It's a commitment to stop respecting and evaluating people based solely on what we think they should accomplish, and start respecting them for who they are, and holding them accountable for what they're actually doing."[2]

Whether you buy that people are doing their best or not, hope is built on doing our part to make the world better. Useful fictions can be a tool to help us get there.

Reflect

Do you believe most people are doing their best? Why or why not? What are the consequences, positive and negative, of this perspective?

Practice

For one day (or a week, or more!) be aggressive in assuming good intent on the part of others and notice what happens within you. (Cautionary reminder: Useful fictions are not a blanket license for others to harm or abuse us.) Write some useful fictions for yourself. Consider the question, "What would need to be true in order for me to respond at my best?" Then act as if it were true.

The Practice of Pulling Up the Anchor

THESE ARE NOT YOUR parents' playgrounds. Featuring natural materials, movable features like dirt and water, and climbing structures resembling immense abstract art, they're a world away from the standard swingset-and-monkey-bar combo that many of us grew up with—and thank goodness. Many communities are recognizing that children today have much more structured time than ever before, and fewer opportunities to experiment and take risks in a safe setting. Innovative playgrounds that deviate from the prefab can allow kids to explore in age-appropriate ways. (Plus those metal slides were real butt-burners.)

I read about these new playground designs and thought instantly of a concept in design thinking called the anchor problem. An anchor problem occurs when we frame a problem in a way that presupposes a particular solution. We want to avoid anchor thinking as much as possible because it severely limits our options and stifles creativity. Dave Evans, a teacher of design thinking, fell prey to anchor thinking in his own life when he moved from a larger house to a smaller one. His first home had a two-car garage that he turned into a workshop; over a number of years, he'd configured it exactly as he wanted. When he moved to a smaller house without the big garage, he took the image of the big workshop with him. It kept him stuck in inaction for years, without any kind of workspace, until he realized he'd been anchored to an image of how it "should" be and needed to let that go.[1]

The new trend in playscapes reflects just that kind of creativity. Anchor thinking would be, "We've got open space and kids; we need a playground for them." On the surface that doesn't sound problematic. Except most of us, when we hear the word "playground," probably picture a playground like the ones we experienced as children. Designers of the new playscapes, by contrast, define their challenge completely differently, free of anchor thinking. They ask other questions. "How can we create an environment that encourages free play, improvisation, and problem solving?" "How do we invent a structure to combat the increasingly structured and programmed lives of children?" With different questions, they're not anchored to a particular solution or design.[2]

It's natural to engage in anchor thinking, especially when faced with uncertainty. The past is a huge anchor—we can't imagine the future, and what we do imagine seems scary, so we default to what we know. It's why churches, the organizations I know best, so often define success using markers of the past: full pews, a thriving Sunday School, a hefty youth ministry calendar, a burgeoning choir. What would it look like to de-anchor from these vestiges of the past and step into an uncertain future?

Forward-thinking institutions are rightly asking themselves how to adapt to an ever-changing world, with the recent pandemic hastening the conversation. Individual organizations need to figure out what the future looks like in their contexts. But if our post-COVID world looks like it did pre-COVID, we have failed this moment. Some semblance of "normal" may be possible, but the danger lies in putting "back to" in front of it. "Back to" is an anchor. There's no going back. For churches, everything can be up for grabs: membership, attendance, worship, connection, mission. All of these things are potentially impacted and will need to be reimagined.

In his book *Lost Connections*, Johann Hari tells the story of a farmer in Cambodia who worked in the rice paddies until he lost his leg from an abandoned landmine. He was outfitted with a prosthetic leg, which caused a great deal of pain when standing in the water of the rice paddy each day. The man struggled more and more, eventually becoming depressed.

Western doctors might have put the man on antidepressants, but the doctors in Cambodia handled it differently. They spoke with the man in depth, understanding his trauma and the physical pain he was in, and its impact on his work. They asked, "What about dairy farming?" They bought the man a cow and helped him make the transition to a life that didn't involve a physically painful and emotionally retraumatizing location. Within a few months, the depression was gone.

Antidepressants are absolutely the right solution for countless people. But I'm struck by the wisdom of the man's community to help him get beyond anchor thinking.[3]

This is hard, scary, and tiring work. It's much easier to slap up a prefab playground and be done with it. And maybe, sometimes, good enough is good enough. But eliminating anchor thinking is a skill that can be developed, and it's a feature of hopeful living as well. We've said that hopeful people engage in pathway thinking, the ability to think through multiple solutions, and agency thinking, the belief in their own empowerment to make a change. Casting off the anchor can help lighten our load for a new, hopeful approach.

Reflect

"Forward-thinking institutions are rightly asking themselves how to adapt to an ever-changing world." How are organizations to which you belong doing this work? Where do you see room for improvement? How might you be part of that adaptive work?

Practice

Identify some of the anchors you carry. How might you reframe them?

6

Hope Beyond Hope

"The only kinds of fights worth fighting," says journalist I. F. Stone, "are those you are going to lose, because somebody has to fight them and lose and lose and lose until someday, somebody who believes as you do wins."[1]

Loss is inherent to hope. We don't always see the results of our efforts.

And so, part of hope is perseverance—perseverance when things don't work out, perseverance when we aren't "feeling it."

How do we have hope for the long haul?

Is hope even required in order to persevere?

If not, how do we find what we need to carry on?

～

Hope as Protest

~~~~~~

IT WAS A STUNNING Tuesday morning in September. My seminary classmates and I were sing-songing our way through the Hebrew alphabet when we heard the news that two planes had crashed into the World Trade Center. In the shock of the hours and days that followed, things went on mostly as scheduled, though with minimal academic content— classes focused less on the Great Schism or the mechanics of a good sermon and became an excuse to huddle together. The convocation ceremony took place as planned on September 12, though the day was less festive, the finery much less fine.

On the seminary community bulletin board, called the Wailing Wall, a few students lamented that classes were not canceled, that we had continued with "business as usual" during a national tragedy. At the bottom of the note, a professor scrawled a response: "Martin Luther said, when the world is falling apart, plant a tree. We were planting trees." *Yes,* I thought, as a tenuous hope shivered its way up my spine.

Unfortunately, the quote is apocryphal. Luther never said to plant. But the biblical prophets did. Jeremiah, for example, speaks to a people under foreign rule, in a foreign territory, having been driven from the land their God had promised and provided. But Jeremiah's message is infused with a rash, ridiculous hope. "Build houses here," Jeremiah says, "and live in them. Plant gardens and eat what they produce." And as impossible a task as it may seem, "Seek the welfare of the city where I have sent you into exile . . . in its welfare you will find your welfare" (29:5-7).

Colloquially, we often use the word "prophet" as a synonym for prognosticator, someone who can predict the future. But Jeremiah had no foreknowledge of an end date to the exile, nor whether that end would even come. What he had was hope and a willingness to act as if that hope had already been realized.

Some time ago I was cleaning out a chest of drawers and stumbled upon a box of cassette tapes from a 1996 conference on peacemaking. Suddenly I was a young adult again, just beginning my journey toward seminary. I had gobbled up every lecture, every workshop, every animated conversation in the dining hall about things that mattered—immigration, LGBTQ+ justice, nuclear disarmament, poverty, racial and gender equity, environmental justice. It was as if Jesus himself were giving me marching orders into ministry—and making clear what that ministry was to be about.

One speaker, the Trappist monk Paul Jones, made such an impression that I played his tape again and again that summer, committing many of his words to memory. He spoke of his decision decades earlier to commit to the way of Jesus, a decision made over coffee and scripture, specifically the book of Revelation's vision of a new heaven and a new earth. It's a vision of a restored creation in which every tear has been dried from every eye. Jones found that vision so beautiful, so compelling, that "I made a decision [that day] to gamble my life in commitment to that dream. And if there is a God—and I pray to God that there is a God—then my life will be a co-creator of that vision. And if there is no God"—and here his voice curled into a fist of defiance—"then my life will be an undying protest against the non-existence of God."

I don't even have a working cassette player anymore to see whether I remember his speech correctly. Honestly, I'm not sure it matters, because his words are my words. I, too, pray to God that God exists, though many days I will settle for a vague sense that all of this is heading *somewhere*. Yet we live in a society in which fewer and fewer people claim a religious tradition of any kind—let alone the way of Jesus, the tradition I stubbornly claim. Given what often passes for religious witness in our country, with its petty squabbles, mean-spirited excesses, and frequent collusion with the ugliest expressions of power, I can't say I blame the slow exodus out the door.

In the wake of the injustices and indignities plaguing us, living my life as undying protest seems feeble. But it's a way of joining with prophets like Jeremiah, of participating with his insolent no against the idea that God's people would be forsaken and adrift forever. Some days, I don't feel hope. But you don't need to feel hope in order to stand up and say no.

Reflect

We often think of hope as a striving toward a particular positive outcome. In what way is hope also a protest?

Practice

Many of us are familiar with the "In this house we believe" signs, with all sorts of positive affirmations. As a twist on this idea, make yourself a protest list: where are your lines in the sand? Where does your conscience compel you to say no? How do these protests help you embody hope more fully, or get along without it?

HOW DO WE PERSEVERE even when we don't feel hope? Where do we find our sense of "normal"? And what happens when the immediate crisis subsides but the world has changed right under our feet?

A while back, I was introduced to three terms, often used in finance, that help describe these shifts and how we weather them.

The first term is *disruption*—the idea that many of our usual ways of doing things are temporarily suspended, but once the immediate crisis passes, we will go back to "normal."

The second term is *displacement*, where the crisis doesn't just disrupt life, it actually shifts stuff around. There's no going "back" when the crisis passes; you're in a new place and you have to find new resources and fresh ways of doing things.

The third term is *destruction*—the most self-explanatory but also the most painful. Some aspects of Life Before will not return.[1]

I think about these words in terms of crossing a river. Disruption would be traffic on the bridge—we may have to wait a while, but once things clear out, we can proceed as usual. Displacement is when we discover our favorite bridge is closed, and traffic is being re-routed to another bridge way down the road. Now we're delayed, and maybe there's a toll we didn't expect, and the usual place where we stop for ice cream isn't on the way anymore, and the kids are cranky in the backseat. But hey, at least we've arrived, only not really, because the detour puts us in a totally different town.

Destruction: the bridges are all washed out. We must swim, build a ferry, or learn to be content where we are.

Health crises, marital issues, job losses—every major transition in life has the potential to be an uproarious mix of disruption, displacement, and destruction. Our country's necessary and overdue discussion of our racial history has bits of all three.

How does hope interact with each of these shifts? When faced with disruption, hope can be swapped out with patience. The hard times will end; good times will resume; if we sit tight, we will weather the storm. Displacement requires a more intentional sort of hope. We can't simply wait for the tough stuff to end; we are invited to take action: scanning the horizon for viable options, working collaboratively, engaging in faithful experimentation.

Destruction calls forth the most robust hope of all, a belief that something redemptive can emerge from the smoking rubble. Many observers wring their hands when Black Lives Matter protesters take to the streets and property is damaged. "Such destruction," people say with a shake of the head. Yet the real destruction goes way back and cuts much deeper: destruction of native peoples and lands; destruction of cultures through the kidnapping and enslavement of generations of Africans; destruction of dignity and livelihoods through Jim Crow laws, redlining, police brutality, and mass incarceration. The centuries-old trauma and despair are real. While I stop short of celebrating vandalism, I'm loath to pass judgment on it either: such outbursts come from a place of deep lament, and generations of harm in communities for whom justice has too often been denied. I can't help but cling to an almost reckless hope that the unrest is pointing us toward something—that the wreckage of our current age might yield something equitable for communities of color and more humane for us all.

In exploring these three ideas with church leaders, many have sought to reframe these financial terms theologically. The scripture has its fair share of temporary disruption, though the bulk of the story seems to be a series of displacements: the exodus of a people from enslavement, the exile into a foreign land, the nomadic ministry of Jesus, the missionary journeys in the early church. And there's plenty of straight-up destruction too. The temple in Jerusalem is leveled and rebuilt multiple times. Kingdoms rise and fall. But Christians, at their best, do not believe in wanton, purposeless destruction. Destruction is often essential for new things to emerge. I love Frederick Buechner's reminder that in the Christian story, the worst thing is never the last thing.[2] We can "cheat" and skip Good Friday services, and just attend Easter if we want. But Jesus couldn't be resurrected without dying first. That yes has no significance without the force of the world's no trying vainly to assert itself.

Reflect

Where do you see disruption in the world around you? How about displacement? Destruction?

Practice

"Destruction is often essential for new things to emerge." When you see examples of destruction in the news or in your own life, be on the lookout for something new to be created out of the ashes. It doesn't always happen, but when it does, we don't want to miss it.

In Praise of Slow and Sloppy

~~~~~~

EVERY YEAR, THE FIRST-YEAR CLASS at the US Naval Academy in Annapolis, Maryland, attempts the traditional Herndon Monument climb, a problem-solving and team-building activity in which the group must scale a twenty-one-foot obelisk coated with water and grease. The objective is to remove the plebe's hat perched on top and replace it with the midshipman's cover, which is the upper-class-person's hat.

In 2021, it took the group three hours and forty-one minutes, the second slowest time in recent history. Only the class of 1998 took longer, at just over four hours. Onlookers could tell it was going to be a long day. The group struggled to get organized and had a setback when they knocked the plebe's hat off the monument, only to be told that it must be dislodged with a human hand, not a projectile.

But the elation at finally meeting the challenge was palpable. "We are the COVID class," yelled student Michael Lancaster. "We've beat COVID! We beat Herndon! And we are plebes no more!"[1]

There's something impressive about being the quickest and breaking records. Anyone who's watched elite runners surging at a marathon finish line knows this to be true. But for sheer drama, inspiration, and grit, I'll take the back-of-the-packers any time. These are the folks who keep up the fight after the water stations are packed up and the cheering crowds have thinned or disappeared, who have to problem solve against the heat of the afternoon or the blisters on top of blisters.

And if the Herndon climb is truly a learning exercise, then a group that takes a long time to finish is going to gain more useful wisdom than groups who fall immediately into a strategy that works. The 2021 plebes experienced discouragement, setbacks, and failed attempts. They had to regroup and shift roles. (Lancaster had been hanging back earlier in the day, only to scramble up the pyramid in the end.)

I'm a sucker for slow and sloppy, having seen my own kid advance, fall down, get up again, scramble, fall, and persevere some more. There were times when Caroline's graduation from high school seemed in grave doubt. But we made it. Still, graduation was a bittersweet time for me as a parent. We love to celebrate the cream of the crop, whether in the social media humblebrag or on the graduation dais. We're not as good at honoring those who overcame much. Often we don't even know their stories. But I know the story in my house, which is of a child who completed high school well and on time despite grueling headwinds, who learned to ask for and accept support, find a sustainable pace, practice self-care, and have perspective on what matters and what doesn't.

But it took a toll. We don't know what the future holds for Caroline. Nobody does. But like those plebes at the Naval Academy, my kid made it up that Herndon Monument in messy, slow, world's okayest fashion.

And the future may be brighter not despite a tough slog but because of it.

Reflect

Reflect on the tough slogs in your life. How have they shaped and instructed you? (It's also OK for difficult times not to yield life lessons. Do not force this.)

Practice

Make "World's Okayest" your mantra. For just a little while—a day, a week—practice believing that good enough is good enough. Notice what happens when you do.

Persevere, Rest, Persevere

~~~~~~

ONE OF MY FAVORITE running workouts is a track workout called rest roulette.

The workout involves a series of 400s (one lap, about a quarter mile) at a fast pace. When you're done with the 400, you push the lap button on your watch, which will record the stats for that interval of running. Whatever the last number is, you multiply it by twenty, and that's how many seconds of rest you get before the next 400. For example, if the first lap takes 1:38.26, take 6 x 20 = 120 seconds of rest.

It's a mental exercise as much as a physical one. The higher the digit, the more rest you get. During a recent round of rest roulette, I got pretty lucky with a few sevens and eights, but I also got a few fours, and my last round ended in a one: only a twenty-second rest. (At least it wasn't a zero.)

Around the second or third round, it stops being about running and starts being a metaphor for life—running hard, resting when possible, then doing it all again, never quite knowing when the next sprint will begin.

Life comes at us pretty fast. There's little time to breathe, let alone process. A colleague described our lives as bodysurfing in the ocean, getting hit by a wave, and having another one strike while we're still flailing and sputtering. Job stress piles on top of a parent's declining health, on top of an expired license plate, on top of a busted refrigerator.

Hope requires steadfast effort, but not at predictable, measured intervals. There's only one thing to do in such times. It's what gets me through rest roulette: run by feel, paying attention to your body first and foremost.

In the age of GPS watches and fitness trackers, runners can become addicted to tracking the stats, comparing present performance to past efforts, and pushing ourselves way too hard for the sake of a number on the watch. But rest roulette helps us listen to our bodies: what we're feeling and what we're capable of *right now*. I'm not going to run as fast after a short break as a long one, and that's as it should be.

I recently took a day-long drive which involved several hours of torrential rainstorm. My passenger and I would barely escape one band of showers before entering the next. At one point, I was poking along behind a semi-truck, hazard lights flashing, my wipers barely keeping up with the onslaught. I fixed my sights on those faint red taillights, my only visible guide. Occasionally, they vanished from view, as if the truck had eerily disappeared into the mist.

For a while, I asked my companion to check the radar to see what was up ahead. *OK, just a few more miles, then a break in the weather.* I soon realized that knowing how long the rain might persist was distracting me from the act of driving. I needed to adjust my thinking from "how much longer will I need to do this?" to "I'm in this for however long it lasts." No conversation, no investigation. Just this moment, for as long as necessary.

I have a weekly check-in with my friend and fellow coach LeAnn Hodges in which we take turns coaching each other. She shared that on a recent Monday, she found herself with an abundance of energy and a positive outlook. By Friday she was scraping the bottom of the barrel, completely depleted and pessimistic. So she took the weekend to putter, spend time with family, and have some creative fun. By Monday she was full again.

It would have been easy, perhaps, for her to feel disappointed for ending the week so much lower than she began it. But in a world as chaotic and broken as ours, hoarding energy is a luxury we can't afford; there's too much work to do. Instead, she realized she had exactly the energy she needed, used it well, and used it all—and was present enough to know when it was time to refill the tank. This kind of self-awareness takes a lot of attention and intention—and she'd want me to tell you, she miscalibrates and ends up overdrawn on occasion, as do we all—but it's a necessary skill amid everything we face right now.

I have a complicated relationship with the phrase "do your best." It's meant to convey grace and compassion: "Honey, give yourself a break. You're doing your best." But in my head, I can always imagine a best that's better than my current output. I've had to nuance the phrase for maximum self-kindness: "This is *today's* best, and that's OK."

Today's best doesn't need to be pretty. Hope is robust enough to survive it. We get through today, world's okayest style. And then do the same thing tomorrow.

When I ran the Houston Marathon, a mantra came to me: *Keep doing this.* Not very poetic, I suppose, but it helped me finish strong that day and many days since. "Keep doing this" means don't get fancy. You know what it takes because you're already doing it. Persist—nothing more.

Reflect

"I needed to adjust my thinking from 'how much longer will I need to do this?' to 'I'm in this for however long it lasts.' No conversation, no investigation. Just this moment, for as long as necessary." What does this idea evoke in you? Do you find this kind of presence easy or hard, or does it vary? What accounts for the variance?

Practice

The practice for this reflection is simple but not easy: rest. For however long you can manage it.

MY FATHER DIED suddenly during my last semester of seminary. I had just negotiated my first ministry position and was days away from having my first baby. Selling our house, buying another one, graduating, moving cities, and starting the job were still to come in rapid succession.

Dad's death cast a shadow over what would have been a happy, albeit stressful time. There was so much to process emotionally. A few days after the memorial service, I made a decision, or perhaps it was simply a realization: *I cannot deal with this grief right now.* I put it all in a box and tucked it away in my heart, which was broken but still needed to keep beating for the sake of my child still to come and the transitions that would follow. I knew there'd be a reckoning, a time that the box would burst open and its contents demand to be dealt with. That moment came to pass months later and landed me in therapy for a long blessed while.

I'm not sorry I partitioned my grief this way. I don't second guess how it all went down. Sometimes we simply have to get through certain periods of our lives. But as I age, I'm learning to cherish the distinction between *getting* through something and *moving* through it.

When I think about that time of my life, I remember a lot of joy: the way our daughter changed day by day, the excitement of choosing our first house as a family of three, meeting the congregation that would come to love me as their own, and vice versa. But then I consider the grief, and I flash to a scene from a war movie, like I'm barreling through no man's land, hoping I miss the mines and the snipers miss me. Getting through was a brute-force motion, a hunkering down, a squaring of the shoulders. "Just do what you need to do," we often say.

Moving through is something different, starting with how it feels in my mouth. Getting through is a gritting of the teeth. Moving through is a two-word poem, with soft consonants, and vowels you can draw out as long as you wish.

During dark nights of the soul, we are like the psalmist, waiting like those who watch for the morning. But the dawn doesn't come to us. Rather we move *into* the dawn, simply by virtue of being on the revolving earth. The light is fixed; we are the ones who shift. No, time doesn't heal all wounds. But "moving through" leavens our experience with a lot of grace. Even if we do nothing, the ground under our feet is moving us, and there's little we need to do but pause. When I was a child in Houston, people would say, "If you don't like the weather in Texas, wait a minute."

Most things in life are like the weather in Texas.

As part of Caroline's high school graduation celebration, we invited grandparents and other family to share the answers to two questions: "what do you know for certain?" and "what is still a mystery to you?"

The mysteries were delightfully varied, but most answers to the first question were variations on "this too shall pass." For these wise elders, moving through often means trusting the passage of time.

In a recent conversation, trauma specialist Bessel van der Kolk talked about how different cultures cope with suffering. In Northern European and US cultures, he quipped, we typically talk or we drink (or take medication). Other cultures move their bodies together more than we do. "We're not very good at singing together and moving together," he says. "You go to China after a disaster and people are doing qigong together, and so that's interesting, or tai chi. And you go to Brazil, and you see people practice capoeira. [And you think], are they practicing capoeira because it looks good to the tourists, or are they practicing capoeira because it does something to the way they relate to their bodies and their sense of self-control?"[1]

Exercise helps us move through. So does tending a garden. Calling a friend. Taking action for others. Dancing. Sometimes, not always, we look up from our movements to discover the thing that "too shall pass" has passed. We usually don't notice it until we're looking back, though. In the moment, things are better, then worse again, then better. And they're only marginally better, imperceptibly better. And then, 1 percent better than that. Or 0.01 percent.

Moving through needn't be dramatic; it can also be subtle. Movement includes the motion of our belly up and down as we breathe, unable to do anything else. Or the sense of being carried along by friends.

After civil-rights pioneer John Lewis's death in 2020, I delighted in the videos that were shared of him in the latter years of his life, full of hard-won joy, and often dancing or moving his body in some way. My favorite is of a seventy-six-year-old Lewis, crowd-surfing on a late-night talk show. When a journalist asked him about it later, he said, "It was amazing. I just wanted people to keep me up. . . . I've been beaten and arrested and jailed a few times. So [I figured I'd] just go with the flow. I thought it would be OK. And it did work out."[2]

Reflect

Consider the difference between getting through and moving through. What does each phrase connote?

Practice

What helps you move through? Practice some of that this week.

Go until No

WHEN SEPTEMBER ROLLS AROUND, I know it's time to get ready for another Ragnar Relay. Ragnar is an event in which teams of twelve people take turns running for some two days straight, through day and night, rain and shine, cold and heat. For several years I've captained a team of runners who make the trek from Cumberland, Maryland, to Washington, DC, a distance of two hundred miles. Each person runs three legs, for a total of thirteen to twenty-plus miles. As each runner completes their leg, vans carry the other runners to the next checkpoint, along with a considerable amount of gear and snacks. When the previous runner reaches the checkpoint, that person tags the next runner, and off they go.

Every year as I prepare for Ragnar, I smile to remember 2015, when we made our race preparations with one eye on the Weather Channel. Hurricane Joaquin was wreaking havoc on the Bahamas and threatening the mid-Atlantic—exactly where we'd be running in a few days' time. Forecasters were having a hard time predicting exactly where Joaquin would make landfall, but it looked like we were in for a soggy race. Rain we could handle, but what about winds? Flying debris? Flash floods?

One member of the team was blunt: "I have serious concerns about doing this race." Another jumped in to agree. Others weren't sure. They were willing to try it, but this is a team event, and they didn't want to appear to be strong-arming the reluctant folks. Besides, wouldn't Ragnar personnel cancel such a large endeavor if it were unsafe? They had to be watching the weather at least as closely as we were.

Finally, as captain I needed to make a call. "Anyone who feels uncomfortable with moving forward is welcome to back out with no hard feelings," I said. "We'll miss you, but we'll muddle through. But as a team, we're going to proceed until it becomes clear we shouldn't. We don't have enough information to make the call to cancel. Things could work out fine. Or we may reach a decisive point at which it's unsafe (or no longer fun), at which time we'll stop. I trust that we'll recognize that point when we get there. Until that time, we are moving forward."

So we packed our vans, just like we'd planned, and we headed to Maryland. Only one of the thirty-six legs ended up being canceled due to high water. The rest were soggy, and some were cold. But we completed the relay. One foot in front of the other, one runner at a time, with a van leapfrogging our path, we did it.

I call this approach "Go until No." It happens often in life, that we have to make a decision without the whole picture. My natural inclination is to stay put until I work out all the details so I can make a risk-free choice. Or I preemptively say no to an exciting possibility if there's a chance it won't work out. But sometimes we don't get the full picture *until* we commit ourselves and take a step forward. As has been attributed to St. Augustine, "solvitur ambulando": *it is solved by walking.*

"Go until No" requires you to believe that your intuition will tell you what you need to know even if it hasn't yet. It requires you to have trust in the future—not that things will work out the way you hope, but that the future will provide the clarity you need to either keep going, change direction, or turn back.

I've had plenty of people come and go on my Ragnar team over our years together. But it's significant that of those twelve runners in 2015, a majority of them have been back every year since, with only a couple missing here and there due to unavoidable conflicts. Certainly, doing something irrational under adverse conditions—and living to tell the tale—bonds a group like few other things do. But I also like to think we grew closer because of our commitment to "Go until No." What we did was take a leap into the unknown together—and we not only survived but we thrived. For two hundred miles.

Reflect

When have you experienced "Go until No"? What happened?

Practice

Think about a situation that feels intractable or complicated. Imagine yourself taking the next step without full information. Notice how that risk feels. What would it cost you to take a chance? Who might support you as you act?

MY SON RECENTLY READ the Lord of the Rings trilogy. It was a wistful experience for me, since he started out with my reading the first book to him, but he quickly tired of the read-aloud pace and commandeered the book before we could finish.

Like the rest of the family, James is a big fan of the early 2000s Lord of the Rings movies. I enjoy hearing him critique the similarities and differences between the books and the films.

One day he asked me, "What's the difference between 'shall' and 'can'?"

Now, as a Presbyterian pastor, I've attended more than my share of church governance meetings, many of which involve endless debate over policies, including the nuances of "shall," "can," "will," and "must."

I responded, "Buddy, I was made for this moment."

I asked for some context, and he described the scene, which I remembered well from the first movie: a dramatic fight between the wizard Gandalf and a shadow creature called the Balrog. Gandalf ends up holding the monster at bay so the rest of the fellowship can escape to safety. Gandalf falls into the abyss with the Balrog, and it's not clear until the second film what has become of him. (Something wondrous, but that's another topic.)

In the book, Gandalf says this to the Balrog: "You cannot pass ... I am a servant of the Secret Fire, wielder of the flame of Anor. You cannot pass. The dark fire will not avail you, flame of Udûn. Go back to the Shadow! You cannot pass."[1]

In the movie, he says much the same thing, except the final line. There
he says, "You *shall* not pass."

Actually, he says,

> YOU!
>
> SHALL NOT!!
>
> PASS!!!!²

"So what's the difference between 'you cannot pass' and 'you shall
not pass'?" James asked.

We agreed that aesthetically, "shall" sounds a lot more authoritative
than "can," and the screenwriters may have changed it for that reason
alone. Substantively though, in terms of meaning, we decided that "cannot" implies the Balrog lacks the ability to pass; "shall" suggests the
creature may be capable, but Gandalf will not permit it. "Shall" is also a
future-tense word, which adds some gravity to Gandalf's stand: *You're
not getting past me. Not now, not ever.*

"Can" is about externalities. "Shall" is about inner resolve.

"Can" is often out of our control. "Shall" emerges from our own
power.

Every so often I read Tim Snyder's slim book *On Tyranny: Twenty
Lessons from the Twentieth Century*. In it, the Yale historian draws parallels
between authoritarian regimes from the past and our current moment
and offers caution and guidance as these movements reemerge around
the world and at home. More than anything, I like to reread it because
it contains simple pieces of advice like "defend institutions," "be kind
to our language," and "do not obey in advance"—essentially, actions required for good citizenship.

Snyder makes the distinction between nationalism and patriotism:

> A nationalist encourages us to be our worst, and then tells us that we
> are the best. . . . Nationalism is relativist, since the only truth is the re-
> sentment we feel when we contemplate others. A patriot, by contrast,
> wants the nation to live up to its ideals, which means asking us to be
> our best selves.

> . . . A nationalist will say that 'it can't happen here,' which is the
> first step toward disaster. A patriot says that it could happen here, but
> that we will stop it.[3]

Patriots, in other words, focus on "shall": namely, the world as it shall be
because we choose to make it so.

When confronted with the world as it is, when addressing the complacency in the system or the inertia in our own hearts, we need to channel movie Gandalf: *you shall not.* You shall not win. We the people have
power. We refuse to let despair and gloom have the last word, and if it
means we go down fighting for what's right, so be it.

But then, maybe taking a stand on "shall" also leads to "can." Maybe
saying what we will and won't permit helps expose how weak and inept
the dysfunctional status quo truly is.

"Shall" is the genesis of hope.

During the height of apartheid in South Africa, the government tried
all sorts of tactics to shut down opposition. They canceled a political rally
at which Archbishop Desmond Tutu was scheduled to speak. Tutu declared that he would hold a church service instead, which wasn't subject
to the same kind of censorship.

That day, St. George's Cathedral in Cape Town was filled with worshippers. Outside the cathedral hundreds of police gathered, a show
of force intended to intimidate. As Tutu was preaching, they actually
entered the cathedral, fully armed, and lined the walls. They took out
notebooks. They began recording Tutu's words.

But Tutu remained undaunted. He preached against the evils of
apartheid, declaring it could not endure. At one extraordinary point he
addressed the police directly: "You are powerful. You are very powerful,
but you are not gods, and I serve a God who cannot be mocked. So,
since you've already lost, since you've already lost, I invite you today to
come and join the winning side!" With that, the congregation erupted
in dance and song.[4]

You shall not pass, Tutu said.

We will not permit it.

Reflect

What do you think is the difference between "shall" and "can"? And what does that have to do with hope?

Practice

What is within your power to change? Go out and make it happen.

AS A PREACHER, there's one gospel story I've returned to more than any other, and that's the story of Jesus stilling the sea during a great storm. As the tempest begins, Jesus is asleep; he continues to slumber as both panic and waves reach their peak all around him. "Do you not care that we are perishing?" the disciples plead. He stands and, with a couple of words, brings the tempest to a halt (Mark 4:35–41).

I've long been chilled by Jesus's next question, asked in the present tense: *Why are you afraid?* The disciples are still afraid—perhaps even more than they were during the storm. Jesus's show of power has done nothing to quell their fears.

It's easy to gloss over that because in the end, the sea is calm: disaster averted. But don't miss the disciples' response.

These disciples, who had traveled the road with Jesus and lived with him and listened to his stories and marveled at his teachings, are left at the end of the story, faces pale and voices shaky as they ask:

"Who then is this?"

Who then is this, who doesn't even panic when the wind threatens to shred our sail and the waves try to beat our boat into toothpicks?

Who then is this, who can scold the wind into silence, who can utter a word of peace into the very depths of the sea?

Who is this? they ask.

But they don't say, "Who is this, who can still the storm?"

"Who is this who can calm the waves?"

Their question says it all: Who is this, that the wind and waves obey?

It's as if they realize: if Jesus can command the waves into silence, he also has the power to stir them up. If God can take the chaos in our lives and tame it, then God can also take what's tame and make it chaotic.

I've been in the storm.

Our whole family knows it all too well.

The wind kicked up, and we realized our kid was drowning. I felt the impact of every wave: each change in medication; each setback; each morning when I'd turn the doorknob of my daughter's room, not knowing what I would find on the other side of it. I prayed and hoped again and again that it would stop, but the storm raged for a long time, and it was terrible.

Let me be clear: God, whoever and whatever God is, did not send that storm. And God didn't choose to keep it going to "teach me something," or whatever thuggish motive people want to put on God when bad things happen.

But there was no getting off that boat. I loved this kid who'd been entrusted to me. And love "bears all things, believes all things, hopes all things, endures all things" (1 Cor. 13:7). During that storm, I realized how much "hope" and "endure" had in common. I would ride out the hurricane, no matter how long it lasted. I would keep turning that doorknob. I would say to my child, again and again, "I will never, ever give up on you."

Lest you think at this point "what a wholly devoted mother she is"—though I hope I am—that was also the year I ran my first ultramarathon.

Yes, running is my own antidepressant, but this was an act of pure, desperate irrationality on my part. It's also an experience I would never trade for everything. Amid all our caring for Caroline, as well as our other kids, I realized I needed something just for me. It was clarifying: my priorities were parenting and training. The race gave me a warped permission to make everything else a distant second.

The race preparation came to mirror the recovery journey our daughter was on. (I would tell people, "I'm training for an ultra, but believe me—it's only the second hardest thing a Dana will do this year.")

I knew the race would be hard, and it was. But I was used to hard.

Running coach David Bidler urges his ultrarunners to ask themselves a question when the going gets tough:

Where would you rather be?

Those moments where everything is moving fast and your heart is slamming into your chest and you're asking yourself whether you can hang on—that is living. Where else would you rather be? Don't check out on it.... Stay with it, because it's what you came for. It is why you are here.[1]

I think that's why the disciples were afraid, present tense, even after the storm subsided. Because this is what they came for: a life following One who could not and would not guarantee them smooth sailing; a life spent in service to something greater than themselves.

Anyway, I finished the race.

Caroline got better.

It might have been otherwise. And the wind could always pick up again.

But we stay with it. We stay in the storm, hard as it is, because that's where love requires us to be.

Riding out the storm together is why we are here.

Reflect

Reflect on your own times in the storm—how it felt, who was there, the moments when you wanted to escape or hide. Remember those moments with grace and self-kindness. Whatever you did or didn't do, you are still here, and that is something.

Practice

Post the words "Where would you rather be?" somewhere you can see them regularly. Listen to what shifts (or doesn't) when you consider the idea that you are where you need to be.

Notes

~~~~~~

Hope Is Not a Prediction

1. Sabina Elena Vaught, *Racism, Public Schooling, and the Entrenchment of White Supremacy: A Critical Race Ethnography* (Albany: State University of New York Press, 2011), 199.

Hope Is Not Optimism

1. Jonathan Sacks, *Celebrating Life* (London: Bloomsbury Continuum, 2019), 175.

2. Chris de la Cruz, "America's Optimistic Spirit Is Killing Us Because We Don't Know What Faith Is," *NEXT Church*, October 30, 2020, https://nextchurch.net/americas-optimistic-spirit-is-killing-us-because-we-dont-know-what-faith-is/.

3. Katie Hanson, "What Exactly Is Hope and How Can You Measure It?," *Positive Psychology*, April 8, 2017, http://positivepsychology.org.uk/hope-theory-snyder-adult-scale/.

Hope Is Not Charging into the Future

1. John Noble Wilford, "World's Languages Dying off Rapidly," *New York Times*, September 18, 2007, https://www.nytimes.com/2007/09/18/world/18cnd-language.html/.

2. Laura Spinney, "How Time Flies," *The Guardian*, February 24, 2005, https://www.theguardian.com/science/2005/feb/24/4.

3. Brené Brown, "What I've Learned from the Work of Dr. Pippa Grange," July 22, 2021, https://brenebrown.com/blog/2021/07/22/what-ive-learned -from-the-work-of-dr-pippa-grange/.

Hope Is Not Toxic Positivity

1. Susan David, "The Gift and Power of Emotional Courage," filmed in 2017, TED video, 16:39, https://www.ted.com/talks/susan_david_the_gift_and _power_of_emotional_courage/transcript.

2. Elizabeth Hagan, *Brave Church: Tackling Tough Topics Together* (Nashville: Upper Room Books, 2021), 21–22.

Hope Is Not Cause and Effect

1. Derrick Weston, "You Can Take the Pastor out of the Church, but You Can't Take the Church out of the Pastor," *Presbyterians Today* (blog), October 18, 2016, https://www.presbyterianmission.org/today/2015/07/24/recov ering-reverend-11/.

2. Tim Fitzsimons, "Forty Years after His Death, Harvey Milk's Legacy Still Lives On," NBC News, November 27, 2018, https://www.nbcnews.com/fea ture/nbc-out/forty-years-after-his-death-harvey-milk-s-legacy-still-n940356.

3. "Here Is the Speech Martin Luther King Jr. Gave the Night before He Died," CNN, April 4, 2018, https://www.cnn.com/2018/04/04/us/martin -luther-king-jr-mountaintop-speech-trnd/index.html.

4. Fred Hampton, "It's a Class Struggle Goddammit!," speech delivered at Northern Illinois University, November 1969; transcript available at LFKS Collectif, https://www.lfks.net/en/content/fred-hampton-its-class-struggle -goddammit-november-1969.

Hope Is Not the Opposite of Despair

1. "Peace Prayer of Saint Francis," Loyola Press website, https://www

.loyolapress.com/catholic-resources/prayer/traditional-catholic-prayers
/saints-prayers/peace-prayer-of-saint-francis/.

2. *The Shawshank Redemption*, directed by Frank Darabont (Culver City,
CA: Columbia Pictures, 1994).

3. Miguel de la Torre, "Keynote," NEXT Church National Gathering,
March 3, 2020, Cincinnati, OH, https://nextchurch.net/2020-national
-gathering-keynote-dr-miguel-de-la-torre/.

4. de la Torre, "Keynote."

5. Austin Channing Brown (@austinchanning), Twitter, August 26, 2020,
4:50 p.m.

6. Christopher Weston, "Black Panther: Yibambe Meaning Explained,"
HITC, August 31, 2020, https://www.hitc.com/en-gb/2020/04/19/black
-panther-yibambe-meaning-explained-avengers/.

Hope Is Not Solace

1. Miguel de la Torre, "Keynote," NEXT Church National Gathering,
March 3, 2020, Cincinnati, OH, https://nextchurch.net/2020-national
-gathering-keynote-dr-miguel-de-la-torre/.

Hope Is Not Future-Proofing

1. World Economic Forum, "The Future of Jobs Report 2020," October
2020, http://www3.weforum.org/docs/WEF_Future_of_Jobs_2020.pdf.

Hope Is What We Do

1. Susan Shinn Turner, "'Prisoner of Hope': Peace Advocate from Bethlehem Visits NC," *Salisbury Post*, April 1, 2017, available on Rev. Dr. Mitri Raheb's
official website, https://www.mitriraheb.org/en/article/1491912435.

Hope Is Outmatched

1. Theresa Machemer, "Cicadas Fall Prey to a Psychedelic-Producing Fungus That Makes Their Butts Fall Off," *Smithsonian Magazine*, May 20, 2021,

https://www.smithsonianmag.com/smart-news/cicadas-fall-prey-drug
-producing-fungus-makes-their-butts-fall-180977776/.

Hope Is Either On or Off

1. Erik Vance, "Find a Little Light This Holiday Season," *New York Times*, November 20, 2020, https://www.nytimes.com/2020/11/20/well/mind/spir itual-guidance-coronavirus.html.

Hope Holds Things Loosely

1. Adam Savage, *Every Tool's a Hammer: Life Is What You Make It* (New York: Simon and Schuster, 2020), 152–53.
2. Jordan Lancaster (@jordylancaster), Twitter, July 24, 2019, 10:07 p.m.
3. Savage, *Every Tool's a Hammer*, 163.

Hope Is the Long View

1. Ta-Nehisi Coates, *The Water Dancer* (New York: Penguin, 2020), 111.

To Comfort and to Care

1. Sarah Bessey, "How Do I Move out of Survival Mode?" *Field Notes* (blog), August 13, 2020, https://sarahbessey.substack.com/p/how-do-i-move -out-of-survival-mode.
2. Mary Oliver, "Wild Geese," *New and Selected Poems* (Boston: Beacon, 2004), 110.

Right of Repair

1. Ali Corona, "Voices: 'Beautiful People Do Not Just Happen,'" *Baptist Standard*, November 7, 2018, https://www.baptiststandard.com/opinion /voices/beautiful-people-do-not-just-happen/.

The Power of Anger

1. Madeleine L'Engle, *A Wrinkle in Time* (New York: Farrar, Straus and Giroux, 2007), 203.

2. L'Engle, *A Wrinkle in Time*, 98.

3. Valarie Kaur, *See No Stranger: A Memoir and Manifesto of Revolutionary Love* (New York: Random House, 2020), 130.

Shock, Silence, Stillness

1. Tricia Hersey, "How Will You Be Useless to Capitalism Today?," *The Nap Ministry* (blog), August 3, 2021, https://thenapministry.wordpress.com/2021/08/03/how-will-you-be-useless-to-capitalism-today/.

2. Emily Dickinson, "'Hope' Is the Thing with Feathers," available on the website of the Poetry Foundation, https://www.poetryfoundation.org/poems/42889/hope-is-the-thing-with-feathers-314.

Trauma = Pain + Confusion

1. Maria Popova, "Why the Best Roadmap to an Interesting Life Is the One You Make up as You Go Along: Daniel Pink's Commencement Address," *The Marginalian*, September 18, 2015, https://www.themarginalian.org/2014/06/25/daniel-pink-northwestern-commencement/.

2. Resmaa Menakem, *My Grandmother's Hands: Healing Racial Trauma in Our Minds and Bodies* (London: Penguin, 2017).

3. Menakem, *My Grandmother's Hands*, 205.

Low-Power Mode

1. Valarie Kaur, *See No Stranger: A Memoir and Manifesto of Revolutionary Love* (New York: Random House, 2020), 197.

Hope Enters the Body through Joy

1. Langston Hughes, "I, Too," available on the website of the Poetry Foundation, https://www.poetryfoundation.org/poems/47558/i-too/.
2. Molly Ivins, "The Fun's in the Fight," *Mother Jones*, May 1, 1993, https://www.motherjones.com/politics/1993/05/funs-fight/.
3. Greg Kandra, "Stephen Colbert: 'If You're Laughing, I Defy You to Be Afraid,'" *The Deacon's Bench* (blog), September 19, 2007, https://www.beliefnet.com/columnists/deaconsbench/2007/09/stephen-colbert-if-youre-laughing-i-defy-you-to-be-afraid.html.
4. John D. Payne, "Tale of Lazarus Shows Us How to Face Death without Fear," *Wichita Falls Times Record News*, June 13, 2020, https://www.timesrecordnews.com/story/life/2020/06/13/tale-lazarus-shows-us-how-face-death-without-fear/5341789002/.

Hope Travels in Story

1. Lauren F. Winner, *Still: Notes on a Mid-Faith Crisis* (New York: Harper One, 2013).

Something to Live For

1. "A Climate Scientist on 'Slaying the Climate Dragon,'" NPR, October 20, 2018, https://www.npr.org/2018/10/20/659122551/a-climate-scientist-on-slaying-the-climate-dragon.
2. "Transcript: Ezra Klein Interviews Bessel van der Kolk," *New York Times*, August 24, 2021, https://www.nytimes.com/2021/08/24/podcasts/transcript-ezra-klein-interviews-bessel-van-der-kolk.html.

Telling the Right Kind of Story

1. Halimah Marcus, "Ted Chiang Explains the Disaster Novel We All Suddenly Live In," *Electric Lit*, April 2, 2020, https://electricliterature.com/ted-chiang-explains-the-disaster-novel-we-all-suddenly-live-in/.

2. Marcus, "Ted Chiang Explains."

3. Van Lathan, "'The Falcon and the Winter Soldier' Season Awards and Finale Analysis," *The Ringer-Verse Podcast*, April 27, 2021, https://www.theringer.com/2021/4/27/22406310/the-falcon-and-the-winter-soldier-season-awards-and-finale-analysis.

4. Daniel Chin, "The New Captain America Will Be Fighting for Something Different," *The Ringer*, April 27, 2021, https://www.theringer.com/marvel-cinematic-universe/2021/4/27/22405915/sam-wilson-new-captain-america-falcon-winter-soldier-ending-analysis.

5. Chin, "The New Captain America."

Shifting the Point of View

1. Suzanne Collins, *The Hunger Games* (New York: Scholastic, 2008), 141.

2. Maria Popova, "Viktor Frankl on the Human Search for Meaning," *The Marginalian*, February 5, 2017, https://www.themarginalian.org/2013/03/26/viktor-frankl-mans-search-for-meaning/.

Proximate Purpose

1. "The Next Right Thing," written by Kristen Anderson-Lopez and Robert Lopez, from the album *Frozen II* (Wonderland Music Company/Walt Disney Records, 2019); see also Kristen Kranz, "'The Next Right Thing' Is Frozen 2's Most Valuable Legacy," *Hypable*, March 25, 2020, https://www.hypable.com/the-next-right-thing-frozen-2-legacy/.

2. Susan Beaumont, *How to Lead When You Don't Know Where You're Going: Leading in a Liminal Season* (Lanham, MD: Rowman & Littlefield, 2019), 127.

Hopeful Stories Need Tricksters

1. *Loki*, season 1, episode 4, "The Nexus Event," directed by Kate Herron, aired June 30, 2021, on Disney+ (Burbank: Marvel Studios, 2021).

2. Miguel de la Torre, "Keynote," NEXT Church National Gathering,

March 3, 2020, Cincinnati, OH, https://nextchurch.net/2020-national
-gathering-keynote-dr-miguel-de-la-torre/.

3. Daniel José Older, "Garbage Fires for Freedom: When Puerto Rican
Activists Took over New York's Streets," *New York Times*, October 11, 2019,
https://www.nytimes.com/2019/10/11/nyregion/young-lords-nyc-garbage
-offensive.html.

Rethinking (Happy) Endings

1. Simon Sinek, *The Infinite Game* (New York: Penguin, 2020).
2. Lee Sandlin, "Losing the War," posted on the official website of Lee
Sandlin, http://www.leesandlin.com/articles/LosingTheWar.htm.

The Practice of Hope

1. Barbara Kingsolver, commencement address given at Duke University,
May 11, 2008; transcript available on the website of *Duke Today*, http://www
.dailygood.org/more.php?n=5140.

The Practice of Pointing the Compass

1. Will Stenberg, Facebook, June 27, 2018, https://www.facebook.com
/wstenberg/posts/10156414314761192.
2. Miguel de la Torre, "Keynote," NEXT Church National Gathering,
March 3, 2020, Cincinnati, OH, https://nextchurch.net/2020-national-gath
ering-keynote-dr-miguel-de-la-torre/.

The Practice of Ten Things

1. Hrishikesh Hirway, interview with Thomas Kail and Lin-Manuel Miranda, *The West Wing Weekly*, podcast audio, April 3, 2018, http://thewestwing
weekly.com/episodes/006.
2. Rick Jones, "Hundreds of Presbyterians Join March to St. Louis' Justice
Center," Presbyterian Church (USA), June 19, 2018, https://www.pcusa.org
/news/2018/6/19/hundreds-presbyterians-join-march-st-louis-justice/.

The Practice of Surviving the Winter

1. Vaclav Havel, "Disturbing the Peace," posted by the Vaclav Havel Library Foundation, May 4, 2015, https://www.vhlf.org/havel-quotes/disturb ing the peace/.

2. Laura Ingalls Wilder, *The Long Winter* (New York: HarperCollins, 1971), 197.

The Practice of Doing It Yourself

1. *Harry Potter and the Prisoner of Azkaban*, directed by Alfonso Cuarón (Burbank, CA: Warner Brothers, 2004).

2. "Christ Has No Body but Yours," attributed to Teresa of Avila, posted at *Catholic-Link*, June 8, 2021, https://catholic-link.org/quotes/st-teresa-of-avila -quote-christ-has-no-body-but-yours/.

The Practice of the Big Three

1. Samuel Wells, "The Words I Turn to in Times of Grief and Distress," *Christian Century*, December 3, 2020, https://www.christiancentury.org/arti cle/faith-matters/words-i-turn-times-grief-and-distress.

2. Johann Hari, *Lost Connections: Why You're Depressed and How to Find Hope* (London: Bloomsbury, 2019), 132.

3. The On Being Project, "Living the Questions—What's Our Communal Equivalent of Rubbing Each Other's Feet?," February 5, 2021, https://onbe ing.org/programs/living-the-questions-whats-our-communal-equivalent-of -rubbing-each-others-feet/.

4. Gregory C. Ellison, "July Practice: The Three Feet around You," The Fetzer Institute, accessed September 19, 2021, https://fetzer.org/blog/july -practice-three-feet-around-you.

The Practice of Writing Fiction

1. Andy Fitch, "Pictures for Many Different Purposes: Talking to Kwame Anthony Appiah," *Los Angeles Review of Books* (blog), May 9, 2018, https://

blog.lareviewofbooks.org/interviews/pictures-many-different-purposes-talk
ing-anthony-appiah/.

2. Christine Kininmonth, "Brené Brown Top Tip: Assume Others Are
Doing the Best They Can," *The Growth Faculty*, February 24, 2019, https://
www.thegrowthfaculty.com/blog/BrenBrowntoptipassumeothersaredoing
thebesttheycan.

The Practice of Pulling Up the Anchor

1. William Burnett and David J. Evans, *Designing Your Life: Build a Life That
Works for You* (London: Vintage Books, 2018), 74–76.

2. Marianne Dhenin, "Free the Playgrounds!," *Reasons to be Cheerful* (blog),
March 31, 2021, https://reasonstobecheerful.world/free-play-playgrounds
-child-development/.

3. Johann Hari, *Lost Connections: Why You're Depressed and How to Find
Hope* (London: Bloomsbury, 2019), 281–82.

Hope Beyond Hope

1. Auden Schendler and Andrew P. Jones, "Stopping Climate Change Is
Hopeless. Let's Do It," *New York Times*, October 6, 2018, https://www.nytimes
.com/2018/10/06/opinion/sunday/climate-change-global-warming.html.

Navigating the Three Ds

1. Jim Baucom, "Crisis: An Opportunity for Change for Your Congregation," video, 1:10:53, Fresh Expressions Course, https://www.fxconnectus.org
/welcome/video-single?content_id=279.

2. Quoted in Adam Hamilton, "The Worst Thing Is Not the Last Thing,"
March 13, 2018, https://www.adamhamilton.com/blog/the-worst-thing-is-not
-the-last-thing/#.YUedR2ZKjlw.

In Praise of Slow and Sloppy

1. Danielle Ohl, "Naval Academy Class of 2024 Records One of Slow-

est Herndon Monument Climbs in History," *Washington Post*, May 23, 2021, https://www.washingtonpost.com/local/naval-academy-plebes-climb/2021/05/23/675b88c4-bbce-11eb-b26e-53663e6be6ff_story.html.

Moving through It

1. "Transcript: Ezra Klein Interviews Bessel van der Kolk," *New York Times*, August 24, 2021, https://www.nytimes.com/2021/08/24/podcasts/transcript-ezra-klein-interviews-bessel-van-der-kolk.html.

2. Jake Miller, "John Lewis: Crowd-Surfing with Stephen Colbert Was 'Amazing,'" CBS News, September 17, 2016, https://www.cbsnews.com/news/john-lewis-crowd-surfing-with-stephen-colbert-was-amazing/.

It's Already Over

1. J. R. R. Tolkien, *The Fellowship of the Ring* (New York: Ballantine, 1973), 392.

2. *The Lord of the Rings: Fellowship of the Ring*, directed by Peter Jackson (Los Angeles: New Line Cinema, 2001).

3. Timothy Snyder, *On Tyranny: Twenty Lessons from the Twentieth Century* (Waterville, ME: Thorndike, 2021), 114.

4. Wallace Chappell, *The Call of God: Selected Sermons* (Author House, 2011), 162.

Stay in the Storm

1. David Bidler, "Mental Training for Ultra-Runners: 3 Tips," *The Distance Project*, August 29, 1970, https://distanceathletics.com/mental-training-for-ultra-runners-3-tips/.